TO DIE WELL

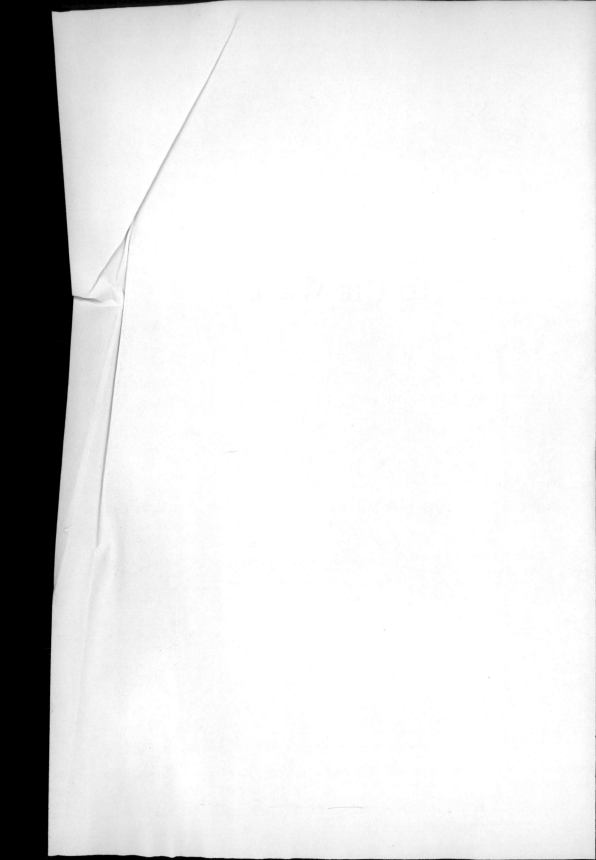

To Die Well

*Your Right to Comfort,
Calm, and Choice in the
Last Days of Life*

Sidney H. Wanzer, MD
Joseph Glenmullen, MD

A MERLOYD LAWRENCE BOOK
LIFELONG BOOKS • DA CAPO PRESS
A Member of the Perseus Books Group

Copyright 2007 © Sidney H. Wanzer and Joseph Glenmullen

Designed by Timm Bryson
Set in 11.5 point Goudy by the Perseus Books Group

Cataloging-in-Publication data for this book is available from the Library of Congress.

First Da Capo Press edition 2007
ISBN-13: 978-0-7382-1083-4
ISBN-10: 0-7382-1083-8

Published by Da Capo Press
A Member of the Perseus Books Group
http://www.dacapopress.com

Note: The information in this book is true and complete to the best of our knowledge. This book is intended only as an informative guide for those wishing to know more about health issues. In no way is this book intended to replace, countermand, or conflict with the advice given to you by your own physician. The ultimate decision concerning care should be made between you and your doctor. We strongly recommend you follow his or her advice. Information in this book is general and is offered with no guarantees on the part of the authors of Da Capo Press. The authors and publisher disclaim all liability in connection with the use of this book. The names and identifying details of people associated with events described in this book have been changed.

Da Capo Press books are available at special discounts for bulk purchases in the U.S. by corporations, institutions, and other organizations. For more information, please contact the Special Markets Department at the Perseus Books Group, 11 Cambridge Center, Cambridge, MA 02142, or call (800) 255-1514 or (617) 252-5298, or e-mail special.markets@perseusbooks.com.

10 9 8 7 6 5 4 3 2 1

Against the complicated setting of modern medicine, life prolongation, and dying, I write this book for patients, families, and caregivers, in an effort to examine what contributes to a peaceful death and what does not. Specifically, the book is dedicated to those patients who did not have a peaceful death.

Contents

CONTENTS

CONTENTS

PREFACE

❧❧❧

I've watched many families struggle with end of life. In this book I describe from my practice what has worked and not worked in the treatment of the dying patient, and I give the reader my observations as to what can ensure, as nearly as possible, a peaceful dying process.

Based on experiences from my practice and interactions with my colleagues, I address the turning points near the end of life when it is time to redefine the purposes of medical treatment. Is the goal to restore health, or is it time to change gears and instead concentrate on shepherding the patient as comfortably as possible through the dying process? Has life become so intolerable that dying is preferable to continued living? These are questions that need to be asked in a formal way with purposeful reasoning whenever a person is approaching the end of life. We shall see that a proper definition of the goals of treatment is critical to a peaceful dying.

This book also explores the ways in which patients and families can work with physicians to maintain control over the manner of dying. There are important questions to ask of physicians, appropriate in a time when the former paternalistic approach by doctors is being replaced with shared decision-making in which patients' and families' wishes are paramount.

I've been able to write this book because of my own experience in the practice of medicine, in addition to work with organizations that promote the rights of the dying patient. I've written on end-of life-issues, and in the 1980s was the lead author of two articles, five years apart, in the *New England Journal of Medicine* on "The Physician's Responsibility Toward the Hopelessly Ill." Co-authored with medical colleagues from around the country, one of these articles stated for the first time in a major medical publication that under certain circumstances it could be ethical to assist in the suicide of a dying patient who was suffering intolerably.[1] This belief, addressed in the chapters on hastened death, I still hold firmly.

The hastening of death in a terminal situation is different from what we usually consider as suicide. Most of the time, we think of suicide as an inappropriate ending of life in a person who is psychiatrically depressed, whereas at the end of life the hastening of death in a situation of intolerable suffering should be regarded more appropriately as part of the whole spectrum of treatment. All of these actions are examined in detail in the chapters on hastened dying.

Many patients or families have graciously allowed me to include their stories in the book in the hope that their experiences might help others. All stories actually happened. Except for members of my own family, I have changed names and places and changed the story in minor ways to protect confidentiality.

Joseph Glenmullen, MD, helped me in the writing of this book through his discussions with me as to what should be in the book, his continuing critiques and suggestions during its writing, and his friendship.

Sidney H. Wanzer, MD
January 2007

TO DIE WELL

Turning Points at Life's End

"What do you mean my mother has had a pacemaker installed to keep her alive?" I asked, aghast at the news. My ninety-two-year-old mother had severe Alzheimer's disease and for years had been imprisoned in an undignified, meaningless existence.

"She developed a dangerous arrhythmia and would not have survived without it," her physician responded.

"But her living will expressly said she didn't want invasive medical procedures!"

At the other end of the phone, her physician was silent. Eventually, he repeated lamely, "She would not have survived without the procedure."

"How could you have violated her wishes?!" I strained at the incomprehensible news. My mother's living will, written long before she lost her mental faculties, made it clear she did not want her dying senselessly prolonged. Installing a pacemaker in this defenseless, ninety-two-year-old woman was nothing short of a massive medical assault. I was astounded. The news seemed unfathomable.

As soon as I was able, I flew from Boston to where my mother had been hospitalized. Nothing could undo the medical travesty that had been visited upon her, but I felt the need to see her, to question her doctor and the nursing home staff further, to do whatever I could to safeguard her wishes for the future. While I was the only physician in the family, my two older brothers shared my indignation over her medical treatment. Our father was spared the anguish over her mistreatment, having died some fifteen years earlier.

All her life, my mother was a fiercely independent, intellectually vigorous woman used to making her own decisions. She was a large woman with a commanding presence—a career professional and mother in the 1930s and 1940s. She was a confident, handsome person whom I remember from my childhood days as being comfortably overweight. She had a wonderful sense of humor that balanced her natural tendency to assert her authority. In addition to raising three sons, she held various executive positions during a long and productive career. Ahead of her time, she was steadfast in her opinions, knew her own mind, and brooked no nonsense from anyone. She was proud of having shaken President Kennedy's hand in the Rose Garden.

One of Mother's more outspoken, well-known opinions was that she did not want her death prolonged if she became physically or mentally disabled and could no longer lead a meaningful, satisfying life. Many times over the years she proclaimed, "If I become senile, just take me out and shoot me." In the 1970s, when living wills first came into use, Mother signed one, clearly indicating that she did not want her death prolonged by medical treatment if the quality of her life ever became so poor that there was no significant intellectual activity or reward. She entrusted the men in her life—my father, my two brothers, and me—with the responsibility for safeguarding this wish.

In 1985, when Mother was ninety years old, she fell getting out of bed and suffered a compression fracture of the spine. By then, she was forgetful and confused at times, a real change from all her previous years of direct and forceful action. After a month or so, it seemed clear to my brothers and me that she could no longer stay in the family home by herself. She and the three of us decided she had to be admitted to a nursing home near one of my brothers.

Following the spine fracture, Mother's ability to participate in medical decisions declined rapidly, but she was initially involved in decision making to the extent possible; we kept her apprised of everything. We made sure that her wish not to prolong her death with aggressive medical treatments was prominently displayed in her medical record at the nursing home. Each time I went to visit her, I spoke with the head nurse, reminding her of the situation. We gave her doctor a copy of Mother's living will and discussed it with him on several occasions. There seemed to be no chance that her life would be inappropriately extended.

After Mother had been in the nursing home for some months, it was obvious she had Alzheimer's disease. Her memory became extremely poor, and she volunteered no opinions about anything (we knew then that she was really impaired!). Her responses to comments or questions were only a few words or less, and her usual strong appetite for books and newspapers had vanished. She simply sat in her chair and looked around the room—her commanding presence was gone. She had lost a lot of weight and had a stooped, hesitant posture. She didn't like to leave her room in the nursing home because she "felt sorry" for all the old people lined up in the hall, sitting in their wheelchairs, looking vacant. Little did she realize that she was just like them. When I visited, Mother barely recognized me. Several years earlier, she would have been aghast to have known what would become of her. The only saving grace was that now she did not realize what had happened.

What to talk about on these visits was always a problem. Conversation was principally a monologue on my part. On one visit, I thought Mother might enjoy a game of gin rummy. For years, she had loved card games, and she and I had played hundreds of games of gin.

"Would you like to play a game of gin?" I asked.

"Yes," she brightened up.

I dealt. Mother picked up her cards and did some arranging of them in her hand. She knew all the motions to go through—

picking up, discarding, making the little noises she always made as the game went on. "Ah! . . . Ummm! . . . That's good . . . Oh, my." Pleased that I had thought of this form of communication, I thought the visit was going quite well. Then, Mother said with a bit of triumph that always went with displaying one's winning hand, "I'll go down now!" She spread out her cards on the table, but there was nothing winning about them at all. No card matched another! All the arranging of cards in her hand, the picking up and discarding, and the murmurs of satisfaction—it all meant nothing. She was truly senile. Mother, as we had known her all our lives, was gone. We "played" another couple hands and quit. I left that visit quite depressed.

The call from her doctor announcing Mother's pacemaker came just weeks after that visit. A nursing aide had been taking Mother's routine pulse and temperature readings, and noted her pulse was only thirty-five, about half of what it normally was. She had suddenly developed a dangerously irregular heartbeat, an arrhythmia. The treatment for an arrhythmia is surgical implantation of an artificial pacemaker beneath the skin. If this is not done, the patient will usually die quickly—within hours or a few days—due to heart failure. Symptoms include profound weakness and shortness of breath. The latter can be treated successfully with morphine, but without the pacemaker, death in the immediate future is fairly certain.

In Mother's case, this would have been the desired end of her indignity. She could have been treated with morphine to relieve any distress, and the unwanted prolongation of her life could finally come to an end. That was exactly the sort of release from her senile imprisonment that she, my brothers, and I wished for her.

Instead, her doctor transferred my mother to the local hospital where a pacemaker was surgically implanted. We were easily reachable for discussing Mother's options, but he had proceeded quickly—without notifying or consulting any one of her three sons.

My mother lived an additional *five years* in a helpless, debilitated state lacking all dignity, totally contrary to her written request. During those five years, she had no quality of life left. Mother never left her room, where she simply stared at the wall. She had no communication with her old friends. Indeed, she would not have been able to recognize them. For the last two years of her life, she needed assistance to go to the bathroom and for all her personal hygiene.

We fired her doctor and engaged the services of another physician who promised that nothing further would be done to prolong her life artificially. Ninety-two when the pacemaker was installed, Mother was ninety-seven at the time of her second and final death.

What Went Wrong

In my mother's case, she had anticipated a turning point in life well in advance, long before Alzheimer's disease had robbed her of her full mental capacities, and her living will was designed far ahead of time to make sure her wishes were carried out. (Now, advance directives, such as health care proxies, discussed later in the book, go even further to protect the rights of patients.) With her living will in place and the many discussions we had with Mother's doctor and nurses, I thought everything was all set. But we made a big mistake. We did not ask her doctor explicitly, Do you agree with this approach and will you promise to adhere to our mother's wishes? He had simply listened to us, and we had erroneously assumed that he agreed.

When my mother was assaulted with a pacemaker, she had not been living for some time; she had been dying. The aggressive medical treatment did not prolong her life; it prolonged her death. The pacemaker did not restore Mother to health, but instead artificially prolonged her dying for five years, an indignity she had expressly stated she did not want to endure.

My Mother's Legacy

My brothers and I never got over the feeling of trespass against my mother, and the experience profoundly affected my actions toward end-of-life patients for the rest of my career in internal medicine. My mother's treatment was so outrageously wrong that it made me vow to try to change things for others. After that experience, I resolved that I would become an activist in promoting end-of-life rights and ensure that those rights were, as nearly as possible, honored. This book is an outgrowth of my experience helping patients and families make health care decisions at the end of life. Over the years, I worked hard to change some of the principles doctors have used in end-of-life care—away from the paternalistic approach and toward the empowerment of the patient's right to choose the type of care wanted at the end of life.

THE FIRST LIVING WILLS

The first activist involvement I had was about forty years ago when I worked with the Massachusetts Committee for the Living Will. In retrospect, it is amazing to see how much opposition there was to the concept of the simple living will in the 1960s and 1970s, something we now regard as a routine matter. The living will stated only what one's preferences were in a document that was to be used as an aid in medical decision making when the patient was no longer able to participate. Yet, the living will was the focus of vigorous opposition by the Catholic Church. I vividly recall testifying before the judicial committee of the Massachusetts legislature on behalf of a law that would recognize the right of the patient to make such statements, at the time tangling with a monsignor of the Church who stated that "it is noble to suffer." However, society's regard for the principles of a living will was slowly and surely changing, and people began to talk about it more and more.

THE MEDICAL PROXY

In 1983, a new concept for protection of end-of-life rights was first enacted into law in California when the durable power of attorney for health care was approved—the medical proxy law. This permitted patients to delegate to an agent the power to speak on their behalf, if they were unable to do so, with the same authority that patients would have had if able to speak for themselves. This was a big advance in protecting autonomy at the end of life, and it was quickly followed in the next decade by similar laws in other states. The living will and the medical proxy are both discussed in more detail in Chapter 12 on legal matters and medical planning.

Doctors Speak Out

In 1989, a group of twelve leaders of American medicine wrote an article in the *New England Journal of Medicine* that outlined the responsibilities of the physician toward the hopelessly ill patient. I do not consider myself to be "a leader of American medicine," but I did organize the production of that article (along with the sponsorship of the Society for the Right to Die). Ten of the twelve authors felt that it could be ethical for a physician to assist in the suicide of a terminal patient who was suffering intolerably, under certain circumstances.[1] This was the first time that, in a major medical journal in this country, such a statement had been made, and it brought about a great deal of attention and discussion.

At the time of its publication, I was on a one-week visit to my boyhood home to say goodbye to a brother who was dying of lung cancer. The storm of media attention that the article generated, resulting from that one sentence in the rather lengthy article, astounded me. For most of the first several days after the publication of the article, I was dealing with calls from newspapers, radio stations, and TV from all parts of this country and abroad—all in the same house in which my brother was dying at that very same time. Those calls persisted in a slowly tapering fashion for a year. It brought home to me how strongly people want ethical and moral approval for the option of ending life when suffering is intolerable. I found myself dealing at the same time with both the abstract principles of autonomy at the end of life and the realities of my brother who at that very time was dying a difficult death.

Similar articles that followed have given moral and ethical backing to physicians who have had discussions with patients about options for an earlier death. Timothy Quill stands out as a physician who courageously detailed and publicized his efforts to aid a suffering patient in 1991 and his own father in 2004 in articles in the *New England Journal of Medicine*.[2]

A Recent Catalyst for the Public's Attention

In 2005, the Schiavo case drew national attention to the tragedies that can occur at the end of life when planning is either not done or is not carried out in practice. The most troublesome problem in the Schiavo case was that no documentation—neither a living will nor a health care proxy—existed to substantiate that Terri Schiavo, a patient living in a persistent vegetative state, would not have wanted her life prolonged. In the absence of such documentation, Terri Schiavo's husband, Michael Schiavo, ended up in a legal battle with her parents, Mary and Bob Schindler, who wanted to continue life support. Eventually, support was withdrawn, and she was allowed to die. But, by the time the conflict erupted in 2005 in the national media, Terry Schiavo had already lived in a vegetative state, with no hope for recovery, for fifteen years!

Proper attention to two turning points in decision making near the end of life can help prevent the problems my mother and Terry Schiavo had. These turning points must be recognized if serious difficulties are to be avoided. That is the crux of this book.

What Are the Two Turning Points at the End of Life?

The first medical turning point near the end of a person's life is the time when the patient turns away from aggressive treatment aimed at restoring health and opts instead for comfort measures to ease the dying process. A second turning point may occur in a very few patients who are suffering intolerably in spite of all comfort measures that are properly administered, such that the patient wishes to hasten dying and thereby shorten the period of suffering. Critically important for this second turning point— that most patients do not need to face, but sometimes do—is the availability of legal options for relief, discussed later in this chapter and in Chapters 8 and 9.

THE FIRST TURNING POINT: OPTING FOR COMFORT CARE ONLY

During most of our lives, medical treatment is aimed at curing illness and restoring health. With our doctors, we push ahead vigorously to try to achieve a cure or improvement. The basic premise is that recovery to a satisfying, meaningful life is possible, and the efforts of patients and caregivers reflect this goal. Treatment may be rigorous, sometimes painful, and with many side effects, but they are justifiable and are usually accepted, when restoration of health is the eventual goal.

With all that our doctors can do now to restore health and prolong life, most of the time we are in debt to modern medicine. However, when cure or significant improvement is no longer possible in a person near the end of life, the goal of therapy should change to that of providing comfort care alone—not prolonging the dying process. This turning point is critical to recognize because, if it is not recognized, inappropriate extension of life occurs.

Only in the last half-century has this decision to change goals become necessary. In the pre-antibiotic era, desperately ill patients frequently succumbed to untreatable pneumonia, and many of the life-prolonging procedures we now consider routine simply did not exist. The situation then was far simpler with regard to decisions about pushing on with treatment. One did everything one could until the end when death mercifully supervened due to natural causes. Now, we have incredible technologies with which life can be medically improved and prolonged. This is progress, but when medical technology is not reined in appropriately, life can be prolonged beyond the point of positive return. The price paid emotionally and physically—and the quality of life—may not be worthwhile, and many of us in this situation might feel we were better off if nature were simply allowed to take its course.

The purpose of medical care at this first turning point should become that of easing the patient through the dying process as painlessly and comfortably as possible. This does not imply less care, but simply redirecting care toward reducing pain and distress, and allowing the patient peaceful last days. This turning point should be defined *before* treatment is begun that might unintentionally prolong life.

Another story illustrates the problem. This story along with that of my mother sets the stage for the rest of the book, which explains the ways patients can avoid these unfortunate situations and stay in control at the end of life.

RICHARD: A LONG DYING

Joseph Glenmullen had a haunting experience with the wrong kind of end-of-life care while working in the emergency department of a community hospital during his training. Like most community hospitals, it drew patients from the practices of nearby physicians and nursing homes. His story follows.

Especially on Friday afternoons and evenings, when the staffs of the local nursing homes would be reduced for the weekend, the ambulances would roll up to the emergency department doors one after another with elderly patients brought for more aggressive treatment than was available at the nursing homes. One of the most common scenarios was that of patients being brought in for aggressive treatment of pneumonia with intravenous antibiotics. These elderly patients typically had severe dementia, often Alzheimer's disease. They had few cognitive abilities left: few memories and little or no idea of who they were or what was happening to them. In the hospital, they would be poked and prodded with intravenous needles. Often, they had to be restrained in the bed because they would not cooperate, their wrists and ankles bound to the bedposts. Their scanty clothing, a thin hospital johnny, was constantly twisting off them as they writhed in bed, exposing their naked vulnerability.

When I was on call, I would be awakened all night long, paged by the nurses to restart IVs these elderly patients had torn out in their efforts to wrestle free of their restraints. As I would restick them with their IVs, all I could think was, pneumonia would be these patients' best friend, a release from their living deaths. Instead, they were subject to a relentless medical juggernaut.

One patient in particular, Richard, has always stuck out in my mind. He was wheeled into the emergency department having fallen out of bed at the nursing home and broken his hip. He had severe Alzheimer's-type dementia; his mind was completely gone; one could not communicate with him in any meaningful way. His arms were gaunt and outstretched, tied to the corners of the hospital stretcher, and his legs were bent at the knees by contractions of what remained of his wasted muscles. Richard looked crucified on the hospital gurney.

Richard's life had been devoid of any quality for years. I assumed he was coming to the hospital for control of his pain from the hip fracture. Imagine my surprise to discover he was being admitted for a total hip replacement! "Why put someone in his condition through such a traumatic surgery?" I asked one of the senior doctors in the emergency ward. "We don't have time to ask those questions," was the reply from the senior doctor as he looked forlornly at the rows of patients on stretchers lined up waiting to be seen. Then he added, with painful resignation, "His hip replacement will be practice for an orthopedic surgery resident."

Looking at Richard, I knew I did not want to live out the last years of my life warehoused in a nursing home, with my brain wasted away, my carcass kept alive by merciless medical treatment, waiting to be used for "practice" in medical training. Nor did I want that to happen to anyone in my family, to anyone I love.

When I heard Richard's story, the phrase "warehoused in a nursing home" jumped out at me. Harsh as it sounds, that's exactly what happened to my mother in the five years she lived after getting a pacemaker. Even before Richard was medically assaulted with a new hip, with his severe Alzheimer's dementia, he had no quality of life left. His was a failed turning point for many reasons: the lack of preplanning, the lack of an advance directive such as a medical proxy, the lack of involvement of family members who could have changed the course of his treatment, and, most of all, the lack of any recognition of the need for a turning point.

In Richard's case, as in my mother's, the doctors became too narrowly focused on treating a diagnosis instead of the patient. Richard was treated as a "hip fracture," and my mother was seen as a case of "arrhythmia," rather than the whole human beings they were. In both instances, nature was not allowed to take its course. Instead, aggressive medical treatment intervened to prolong their dying. This is also what happened to Terri Schiavo, who languished in a nursing home for fifteen years before the conflict between her husband and her parents came to a head in 2005.

The Second Turning Point: A Hastened Death

In rare instances after the first medical turning point toward comfort care only has been reached, even meticulously rendered, maximum comfort care is not enough to control a dying patient's suffering. Under these circumstances, a hastened death is an option some of us might wish to exercise, and it may be the most humane approach. This is done only when death is clearly imminent, anticipated suffering is intolerable to the patient, and all comfort measures have failed.

Due to advanced medical technology, the majority of us will have to take the first turning point at some time in our lives—abandoning aggressive medical treatment in favor of comfort care only. But very few of us will ever reach the second medical turning point of hastening death because modern medicine is so sophisticated in controlling pain or distress. There are few failures to provide reasonable comfort. Still, everyone should be prepared in advance to consider this second turning point should it become necessary. Even in the rare instances in which pain or distress cannot be adequately controlled, some patients will still not want to hasten death. That is their right. Likewise, it should be the right of those who do wish to hasten death to do so, in these rare circumstances.

This second turning point will be discussed in much more detail in chapters toward the end of the book. We shall see that hastening death because of intolerable distress can take several forms, some of them absolutely legal and noncontroversial and some involving the patient's directly taking his or her life, which can be much more complicated legally. As of this writing, in the United States, the latter is clearly legal only in Oregon, where such a death is usually referred to as "physician-assisted suicide."

I prefer the term *physician aid-in-dying* or *hastened dying* because hastening of death in a terminal situation is different from what we normally consider to be suicide, which is most commonly thought of as the act of a person prematurely and inappropriately ending his or her life. By contrast, physician aid-in-dying can be seen as medical treatment, part of the spectrum of options for people suffering at the end of life.

Later chapters will discuss methods of hastening death used by patients in recent years, including methods that are legal and ethical, and also methods that are still evolving in their acceptance by public opinion and our legal system, such as barbiturates (in states other than Oregon) and the growing use of inhaling helium as ways of hastening death for terminally ill patients.

The Importance of Recognizing Life's Turning Points

Planning for and taking life's turning points represent some of the biggest decisions you will make in life. This is true whether you are making the decision for yourself or helping a parent, spouse, or other loved one to make the decision. For this reason, turning-point decisions need to be formal discussions among the patient, family, doctors, nurses, and anyone else who will play a key role in supporting the patient once the decisions are made. Later chapters of this book offer the key issues and questions that need to be addressed to ensure that all aspects of the decisions are considered. These include looking carefully at the patient's diagnosis, prognosis, second opinions, treatment choices, and quality of life—in addition to the various options that can help ensure a peaceful death.

The key to staying in control of one's medical fate is educating yourself about the options, deciding in advance what course you want treatment to take, clearly communicating this to a medical team, making sure they agree to follow stated wishes (or finding others that do), and legally empowering family members to act on your behalf if and when you are no longer able to act because of physical or cognitive disability.

This topic has become politically charged. The Schiavo case demonstrated how the "pro-life" constituency in this country has organized itself against the right to stay in control of the end of life. This has become one of the most hotly contested issues in the national political arena, and has led many people to reflect on their own choices and values. Against this turbulent background, *To Die Well* is intended to provide you and your family with the information you need about the last days of your life.

2

RIGHTS OF THE DYING PATIENT

In order to plan for the best care at the end of life, it is vital to understand your rights as a patient. These are numerous, which most people do not realize. The majority of these rights, which ensure comfort and dignity and allow patients to remain in control at life's turning points, are protected by court decisions that have become established case law, based on constitutional rights and common law. As a result, the rights enumerated in this chapter are legally and ethically not controversial. Every patient and family member should be aware of them.

What Are Your Rights?

Absolute or near-absolute rights, protected by our courts:

- *If you are no longer able to participate in medical decision making, you have the right to have your medical proxy (agent) speak for you with the same authority that you yourself would have if you were still able to make decisions.* This presumes that you have made in writing such a delegation of authority, a subject covered in the chapter on legal matters and medical planning. The appointment of an agent ahead of time is essential if your wishes about end-of-life care are to be carried out.
- *You have the right to have pain and suffering relieved with sufficient medication and vigorous pain management.* This is not codified in law in many states, but it is almost universally agreed upon by

organizations that promulgate national medical standards of practice (e.g., Joint Commission on Accreditation of Health-care Organizations). At life's first turning point, comfort care becomes the focus of treatment rather than restoring health. Even though relieving pain and suffering with large doses of medication can run the risk of an earlier death, pain relief is a priority at this stage in life, and adequate pain relief is essential to ensuring your comfort and dignity. This right is placed under the "absolute or near-absolute" category, although I recognize that it is sometimes not respected. Some doctors are still excessively wary about using enough medication to relieve symptoms, and patients or their agents may occasionally need to insist that this is standard medical practice and must be observed. You should ask your doctor, nursing home, hospital, or hospice what their policies are regarding pain management, since such policies may have a huge effect on your future comfort.

- *You have the right to refuse all unwanted treatment.* This is true even if refusal might bring about death more quickly. The refusal by you or your legally appointed agent of any undesired treatment or procedure is an absolute right. No one can carry out any medical action that affects you without your consent, no matter what it is. The only exception to this might be in the instance of someone administering emergency care to you if you are suddenly not able to speak in your behalf and the attending person does not know your circumstances, or a very special and infrequent circumstance of some sort that has required the intervention of a probate court.
- *You have the right to refuse any unwanted treatment that has already begun.* This can be more difficult psychologically than refusing a treatment before it has been started, but ethically and legally there is no difference between discontinuing an already established treatment and not having begun it in the first place.
- *You have the right to refuse all nutrition and hydration.* This is also an almost absolute right, and it can be of great importance if a

dying person wishes to shorten the period of terminal suffering. Refusing all liquids leads to dehydration and an earlier death. This is discussed at length in the chapter on hastened death.

- *You have the right to refuse cardiopulmonary resuscitation (CPR).* CPR is known as a "heroic measure" in medicine. Most people want heroic measures only when restoring health is the goal of treatment. Insuring this requires special do-not-resuscitate orders in accordance with state public health department regulations regarding emergency care, discussed later in the book.

- *You have the right to change doctors.* Doctors vary in their willingness to discuss end-of-life options, and they vary in their comfort level with patients who want to maintain control. Change doctors if you are not entirely satisfied with this critical member of your health care team. You are a customer who is purchasing a product (health care), and you have every right to choose who provides that care. Sometimes, due to local circumstances, HMO restrictions, or geography, this freedom of choice may not be easy to bring about, but if there is a choice available, you can make it. I have found that patients are often embarrassed to bring up the subject of changing doctors, but they should not be. This involves emotions and personal considerations, but the patient as a consumer has the right to make the decision.

Agreed-upon rights, but not necessarily backed by specific law in every state:

- *You have the right to have valid advance directives considered.* Advance directives are formal, written decisions made prospectively about your end-of-life care, directions that indicate your wishes in advance. Living wills, medical proxy designations, and do-not-resuscitate (DNR) orders are examples that are all discussed in the chapter on legal matters and medical planning. The degree to which they are binding is discussed in that chapter. Living wills, simple statements of your wishes, may or may not be binding. Other forms of advance directives have more legal force. The situation can vary from state to state and situation to situation, although the basic principles are generally recognized.

- *You have the right to be fully informed of all treatment options available to you for end-of-life care.* Ask your doctor about all the options, especially palliative treatment. He or she should inform you of the risks and benefits of each option (whether palliative or curative in aim) as well as the probabilities of treatment success. This is part of "informed consent," which is now the subject of many regulations by governmental agencies and standard-setting groups (e.g., Joint Commission on Accreditation of Healthcare Organizations), plus case law. The doctor has an obligation to inform the patient fully about his or her illness and treatment options and procedures. Not informing the patient fully is substandard medicine.

- *You have the right to know the ways in which undesired lengthening of life can be avoided in situations of suffering at the end of life.* This is discussed in detail in the chapter on hastening death. In a way, it falls under the right to informed consent, noted previously, but you will find few laws or regulations that specifically address undesired prolongation of life. Rather, it is what a conscientious doctor would discuss with the patient. Your doctor should raise this issue, and, if he or she does not, ask about it yourself. If suffering is intolerable despite all efforts directed at relief, you can inquire about legal options for hastening death and not prolonging the dying process. Your doctor—due to personally held beliefs—may not agree to assist in legal ways of hastening death, but you certainly have the right to ask. Organizations, such as *Compassion and Choices* and *Final Exit Network* (both discussed later in the book), can discuss legal options on this subject if your doctor will not. Very few patients actually ever need aid-in-dying, but every patient should think through this critical question in advance.

How Can You Ensure Your Rights Are Honored?

Although the previously mentioned rights are well established and generally not controversial, they are often disregarded, most often because patients and families do not realize what their rights are. Even doctors sometimes need to be reminded and educated about these rights of the dying patient.

There are ways in which people can ensure their rights are respected and their wishes for end-of-life care are met.

- Knowing your rights is basic and most important. You need to be prepared to stand up for them—insist on them.
- Discuss your rights with family and caregivers. Talk about potential problems.
- Always remember that you alone are ultimately in charge of what is done and not done as long as you are competent. This is a very basic concept that confuses many people.
- Make your wishes clear so that you do not leave decisions to others who may make choices for you that you would not want. Indicate your wishes ahead of time with advance directives. This helps you stay in charge when you are no longer competent. If you become unable to make medical decisions, your appointed agent (proxy), speaking on your behalf, can protect your interests. This person needs clear prior instruction by you and needs to act vigorously in your behalf. (Living wills, medical proxy designations, and DNR orders are discussed in Chapter 12 on planning ahead with advance directives.)
- Define goals and stay focused on the goal of treatment—one of the most important ways of ensuring rights are met. Is restoring health the goal? Or, have you reached the turning point where comfort care becomes the goal? If definition of goals is done as a formal exercise, the protection of rights and care of the patient are made much easier.

- Keep treatment in the simplest setting possible (i.e., home, hospice facility, nursing home, and hospital, in order of increasing complexity). The simpler the setting, the more easily rights can be ensured. This dictum tends to be true as long as proper and sufficient palliative care can be rendered in the simpler setting. Sometimes, it might not be possible to get the needed degree of palliative expertise in the simpler setting, and, in this case, one might give up some degree of control in the more complicated setting as the price to be paid for the expertise. In the next chapter on comfort care, we shall see how increasing complexity of treatment increases the difficulty of protecting rights. Most of the time, rights are most easily protected at home when home care is workable and feasible. Avoid transfer to the hospital unless it is clearly necessary for the control of symptoms.

- Ask for a referral for hospice care. The hospice movement has matured greatly in the last twenty years, and expert advice on and assistance with end-of-life problems is now available from hospice units in almost all communities. This does not replace one's usual health care team, but supplements it. Hospice is used to working closely with other health-care providers, and they can provide invaluable help.

The Office Visit: An Older Person Confused about Rights

Alice was a charming woman in her mid-seventies, extremely devoted to her husband George, who had suffered a very bad stroke the previous year. This was evident from the way she spoke of him—lovingly and gently. Her son Wilbur accompanied her to my office, and I was instantly won over by them. The patient himself, too disabled to come with his family, must have been a wonderful man. He had to have been, to have such a wife and son.

Alice had been referred by a psychiatrist colleague of mine who had called to ask if I would speak with them about their options for George at the end of his life. Following the stroke, George had been unable to speak. Communication was reduced to questionably meaningful nods of the head. He choked on food and water and was fed via a gastrostomy tube into his stomach. He had had repeated aspiration pneumonia, which precipitated hospital admissions and antibiotics. He had been in several fine institutions, starting with a famous tertiary center where he was on a respirator, ending with his present nursing home. Whenever George had a threatening fever or respiratory difficulty, he would be rushed back to either an emergency room or a hospital ward for aggressive treatment. He remained totally, completely, and hopelessly disabled.

Alice was confused as to what she should do. She had a properly executed medical proxy that gave her complete authority to speak on her husband's behalf, but she did not really understand that she had that power, and, if she had known, she did not know what to do with it. She was distressed at George's predicament and felt desperately that *something* needed to be done—but was not sure what that could be.

We talked for an hour, and I gave her my thoughts. At the end, as Alice and her son left, both expressed profound appreciation for what I had told them and said that no one in all their multitude of medical contacts had ever spoken to them about my suggestions. They left with new resolve to address George's predicament in a different way—and they seemed relieved and somewhat encouraged.

What had I told them? I discussed what to me were simple concepts and plans of action, none profound or controversial. They were the rights listed previously, all commonsense statements that simply needed to be clarified and understood by the wife and son. I told them not to feel guilt for a firm decision to render comfort care only. George was slowly dying from his stroke, and they were not killing him by saying no to further aggressive intervention. I emphasized that there was no difference, ethically or legally, between a treatment discontinued and a treatment never started in the first place. I urged them to identify the medical person in charge (it needed to be one doctor). Above all else, I pointed out how important it was to work with that person to define the goals of treatment, which were no longer to restore health but rather to provide comfort measures only to ease the dying process.

The rights that exist for patients at the end of life are powerful rights, but they are of no avail if not understood and championed.

3
The First Turning Point: From Active Treatment to Comfort Care

❧

Withdrawing Unwanted Treatment, the First Step

The first turning point, as we saw in Chapter 1, is that time in a dying patient's illness when there is no reasonable expectation of a cure or of restoring health. Efforts now turn solely to providing the care that will keep the patient as comfortable and peaceful as possible through the dying process.

Stopping aggressive treatment aimed at curing the illness is the essential first step of comfort care. This decision can be difficult even when the patient and family realize the turning point has come and agree that comfort care only is the correct approach.

This was illustrated to me by Marie, a woman in her fifties who had cancer of the esophagus. She was a housewife who had raised a family of several children in a suburban town outside Boston and also held a part-time job in one of the retail stores near her home in order to help meet family expenses. Marie was a very hard worker who loved her family and life. Unfortunately, she had been a heavy smoker, and cancer developed in her esophagus—one of many areas where cancers can arise as a result of smoking. Marie had an initial surgery to remove what portions of the cancer could be removed, and then she received radiation. (This was many years ago, and there was no chemotherapy at that time that was thought to be helpful or advisable for that particular growth.)

Marie's cancer recurred and began to block her ability to swallow. She regurgitated food and fluids, which she could not get past the obstruction in her upper esophagus. A small feeding tube was surgically placed through the abdominal wall into Marie's stomach. Through this tube, she received liquid nourishment for a number of weeks during which time she swallowed nothing by mouth—thereby avoiding the obstruction. However, Marie continued to waste away due to the advancing cancer, and she became profoundly weak. Her body chemistry was abnormal. She began to speak very little and to sleep fitfully much of the time. Medications were necessary to control general distress and anxiety, and morphine seemed to work best.

In one of the last real conversations she had, Marie told me and the family, "I want to die, and I want the tube feedings to stop." She said this at just about the time I would have said the same myself, were I in her position. Until then, she could interact with her family and friends to some extent, but now she could do so only with great effort. She had no enjoyment of any part of the day and was bedridden. Marie wanted to be freed from her ordeal and did not want further treatment other than comfort measures. This seemed to me and to Marie totally rational and appropriate, but it was difficult for the family to accept. However, after considerable discussion with the family, and with their approval, I removed the feeding tube, and from then on Marie had no more fluid administered by any route other than the tiny amount needed for intravenous administration of morphine. She quickly became dehydrated, which was not a distress to her in her somnolent condition. The continuous use of fairly large doses of morphine prevented her being aware of any distress. She died several days later, quietly and peacefully.

Marie's tube feeding had become an unwanted treatment and an obstacle to a peaceful and natural death, and at her request it had been withdrawn. That alone sufficed to hasten the end of her suffering. Withdrawing treatment in this situation was accepted by the patient, family, and her caregivers—not happily or easily, but realistically and eventually without reservations.

The stopping of unwanted treatment stands out clearly as the first thing to do when the goal of treatment switches to comfort care only. There is absolutely no legal or ethical problem with this, although it is amazing how many people feel that it is somehow improper to stop a treatment that has already been started. That belief is wrong. There is no difference legally or ethically between stopping any sort of treatment and never having started it in the first place. This includes chemotherapy, surgery, radiation, hormone treatments, or other aggressive measures, plus such simple measures as intravenous fluids or liquid nutrition given through a feeding tube into the stomach.

The decision to withdraw treatment may be difficult psychologically, as well as emotionally. Because it is human nature to worry about stopping a treatment that one has previously had enough faith in to begin. However, if the first turning point has been taken in a formal way through discussions among patient, family, and doctors who agree that it is highly improbable health can be restored, and if the goals have been redefined, this option of stopping a previously initiated treatment should not present a problem psychologically.

What Is Ideal Comfort Care?

In the last decade, palliative (comfort) care has become a specialized form of care in that there is now a defined body of knowledge about what works best. It is something physicians and other caregivers have had to learn. When this knowledge and these skills are put to use, terminal patients in the great majority of instances *can* be kept comfortable.

Optimal comfort care means that the physician will exert meticulous care, attention to the smallest details, close and frequent follow-up, extreme compassion, and the best pain management (the latter is addressed in the next chapter in more detail). Comfort care means paying attention to a myriad of problems that can lead to distress or unease, whether physical or psychological in origin.[1] Because this is now the caregivers' principal obligation, all the emotional energy invested in seeking a cure can be directed to the patient's immediate well-being in an all-inclusive approach—ideally with frequent visits from the physician and other support personnel. Although much of comfort care is common sense, specialized skills may be necessary, and the doctor or patient should not hesitate to ask for whatever consultations are necessary, especially in the area of pain control.

Comfort care does not imply less attention from the doctor. There is an unfortunate tendency on the part of some physicians for this to happen, since, after the first turning point, the more dramatic and appealing attempt to cure the disease is put aside. When this is done, a few physicians are let down when the patient and family decide to abandon attempts to cure, and may tend to "let the nurse or hospice take care of it." Comfort care cannot be regarded as simply something to be done in the absence of more worthy goals.

In my own practice, I was able to give this care personally, whether in the office, hospital, or home—and the location and frequency of visits with the dying patient were my choice. These days you may find it difficult to get the personalized attention from your physician that you desire. There are a number of factors causing this to be true: the highly specialized nature of much of our medical care now, insurance considerations, and the great pressures on physicians to see more patients per day. All work against having your doctor attend you as frequently as you would like, especially at home. Most doctors do not make house calls and the physician consequently delegates more of the care at the end of life to either the nurse or hospice worker. That is a reality I accept but not one with which I agree. Strong advocacy for your needs may solve this to some extent but, most likely, not completely.

To ensure meticulous comfort care, you should consider engaging the services of the hospice movement, which can be extremely important in translating the change in goals into reality. Almost all dying patients can benefit by the involvement of hospice experts. To get the full benefit of the hospice approach, they should be consulted early, as soon as the turning point has been reached and goals have changed. Hospice is discussed in more detail later in this chapter.

Understanding What Symptoms Are Part of the Dying Process

Patients and families need to understand that some happenings are part of the dying process so that the patient who is receiving comfort care is not pushed to fight fruitlessly against symptoms that need to be accepted. Avoiding food, not taking in much fluid, subsequent dehydration, extreme lethargy, sleeping a lot, and the inability to get out of bed are all prime examples of symptoms that naturally occur in the dying process and should not be fought by family, caregivers, or the patient.

I have frequently seen families of dying patients struggle vainly to get the patient to eat more so "you can keep your strength up" or to urge the patient that he must get out of bed because "you will lose your strength." These are useless exhortations for the dying patient and serve only to make the situation more stressful. Acceptance of these symptoms as a normal happening will allow a more peaceful death.

This does not mean that all symptoms that go along with the dying process should simply be accepted—far from it. Many things can happen that can successfully be treated and relieved, while not prolonging dying. For example, breathlessness can be due to a variety of causes, and the symptom is usually treatable. If the underlying cause is not remediable, the symptom itself can be dealt with by morphine, an excellent agent for suppressing the feelings of shortness of breath. Anxiety and panic feelings are often present, and these are clearly responsive to anti-anxiety medications that are quite specific for these particular symptoms. And, as we see in the next chapter, pain is definitely in this category of treatable symptoms.

Drs. R. Sean Morrison and Diane Meier at Mount Sinai School of Medicine in New York City recently wrote an excellent summary of symptom control at the end of life, referring to nausea, constipation, depression, anxiety, shortness of breath, and pain—all being symptoms that mandate the attention of the physician and other caregivers.[2] The bottom line is to accept the first category of symptoms in the dying patient (lethargy, weakness, no appetite, weight loss, and others), as noted previously, but to aggressively address the remediable forms of distress, as described by Morrison and Meier. Discuss with your doctor which is which.

THE LITTLE THINGS ARE ALSO IMPORTANT WHEN ONE IS DYING

Sometimes even the smallest details can be an upsetting problem for the patient, as I experienced recently.

My oldest brother, Bob, died with prostate cancer at age eighty-five in North Carolina only a few weeks before I wrote this chapter. He had this disease for about ten years and was originally treated with radiation. Several years ago, the cancer recurred, and his physicians started him on hormone therapy. Surgery for increasing bladder outlet obstruction by the cancer growth was not a feasible option because of the previous radiation in the area, and some months before his death, he required the insertion of a permanent catheter into the bladder to allow proper urine flow. He began to lose weight rather markedly and felt weak and unsteady, such that he was transferred to the nursing facility of the retirement community in which he and his wife lived. Several weeks before he died, he had a blood transfusion to help correct the severe anemia the cancer had caused, a move that helped his energy level temporarily, but did not alter the basic problem. He made the transfusion decision because there were still a few things he had to do. However, life became distressing not long after that, and Bob appropriately came to the conclusion that he wanted to end his steadily deteriorating state and was ready to die.

I visited him from Massachusetts to say goodbye and to help him formulate an agreed-upon plan for his dying. He had signed a document designating his wife as medical proxy to make decisions for him at a time when he no longer could do so. However, he had not worked out in his own mind a set of clear-cut goals and guidelines except that he and his family knew that they did not want the process to be prolonged.

The day I arrived I was able to talk with Bob while he was still lucid and capable of making decisions. The next day I drew up—with the help of his wife and daughter—a written statement of instructions for his doctors and other caregivers, a statement that set forth the specific wishes that would in his individual case prevent any unnecessary prolongation of his life. This would be an addendum to his previously signed medical proxy document.

The next morning I went over this written version of what we discussed the day before. I read each statement to him and asked, "Is this correct, is this what you want?" For every instruction he said, "Yes." The previous day he had been able to sign a business document, but that day he was no longer able to produce a signature. His wife, who had power as his medical agent, signed for him—and we gave the letter of instructions to his doctors and the staff of the nursing facility.

Bob's document stated that the goal of treatment was to assist him through the dying process with as much comfort as possible. Here is Bob's actual list:

1. Nothing is to be done that will prolong the dying process.
2. No further transfusions are to be given.
3. In the event of cardiorespiratory collapse, no CPR, respirator, or other resuscitative measures are to be used.
4. No antibiotics are to be administered for urinary tract infection, pneumonia, or any other infection.
5. No intravenous fluids are to be given other than the tiny amounts that might be necessary to deliver sedating or pain relieving medications.
6. If dehydration occurs, it is not to be treated by administration of fluids via any route unless I request water to drink, but I am not to be urged to drink fluids.
7. No nasogastric tube is to be used.

    (When patients are dying, they do not want to eat and the desire for fluids becomes minimal or nonexistent. The patient usually will become dehydrated, and this shortens the dying process, usually a good thing. The matter of terminal dehydration is discussed in detail in the chapter on hastening death.)
8. Pain or any other form of distress or agitation is to be treated with medication in sufficient doses to relieve the symptoms, even if the dose required might shorten life. If pain or sedating medicines in intermediate categories do not relieve symptoms of distress or agitation, stronger drugs, such as morphine, are to be used.

    (Addiction is not a consideration in this situation.)
9. There is to be no chemotherapy.

(This was highly unlikely, in his situation, to
have any significant beneficial effect, but, more importantly, Bob said, "I am tired, and I want this ordeal over.")

10. No transfer to hospital is to be made. Dying in the
nursing home is expected and transfer to a hospital
is not an option unless essential for control of
symptoms.

(We tried to be certain the nurses and aides realized that Bob's dying was not a failure of their care,
but rather the desired happening.)

11. There is no need for me to get out of bed or sit up if
I do not wish to do so.

12. No laboratory tests, x-rays, or vital signs are to be
done.

It seemed we had covered everything. There was certainly nothing in the written statement that was controversial, either ethically or legally, and his personalized requests
were things commonly found or implied in standard living
wills. My brother, his wife and family, the doctor involved
in his care, and the nursing supervisor were all perfectly
agreeable to the stipulations.

However, one thing interfered with the execution of the
plan—a holdover attitude of the nursing staff, stemming
from years of habit that seemed to presume we were still at-
tempting to restore a healthier state and to preserve life. Although they wanted to cooperate and in theory agreed with
our approach of shepherding Bob through the dying process
as easily as possible, in carrying out the details they sometimes reverted, subconsciously I am sure, to the restoration
mode. They were giving devoted, conscientious care, trying
their best to do what was right, but it was hard to get away
from the goal of trying to make Bob better and to change instead to the goal of assisting him in his dying. For example,

the staff continued to take Bob's blood pressure regularly, even though the pressure of the pumped-up cuff was very bothersome to him. The staff took rectal temperatures when oral ones became inaccurate, and that was upsetting. Bob's children had to remind each shift of nurses to have all vital sign measurements discontinued. Hospice personnel put into place a nasal catheter for oxygen, in spite of the absence of shortness of breath, and Bob's son had to ask incredulously what they were doing (the instruction for oxygen had been on the routine hospice order sheet). It was discontinued. With regard to water, the nurses continued from time to time to urge Bob to drink, until reminded by his children that they were to give Bob water only at his request.

These upsetting details may seem small, but they were significant. It seemed clear to me that as a generality a lot of education was still needed in order to get caregivers (not just Bob's, but caregivers in all similar situations) to support fully and effectively *in all ways* the patient's wish not to prolong the dying process. I had seen this situation play out many times in my practice, and here it was again in a death in my own family—unintentional, but nevertheless very real. Although it is not easy to do, the underlying approach of all caregivers must change when the turning point has been reached. Until that happens, the family has to remain continuously vigilant to ensure that the patient's wishes are carried out, and the family must advocate for the patient to the very end.

The statement of detailed instructions we developed for Bob (or something similar to it) could be used by any person facing the end of life, either as an optional attachment to the medical proxy document when it is originally signed by the patient—or as a last minute addendum to the proxy statement during the dying process. To ensure that dying will be in accordance with the patient's wishes, I think every dying patient and his or her family should consider drawing up detailed instructions for the final days or week—including the routine matters of care that so bothered my brother as he was dying. The standard living will often does not spell out the details of desired care at the very end.

SETTINGS FOR COMFORT CARE

Delivering proper comfort care and adhering to the wishes of the patient are most easily accomplished when care is delivered in the simplest setting possible—the home.[3] Here, the patient is usually surrounded only by persons who are aware of the goal of care and have signed on to the new guidelines. There are not large numbers of people who must be educated about the situation and instructed repeatedly as to what should or should not be done. Everyone knows and is supportive. The same can be said of a patient who is under hospice care at home where the methods and goals of care are agreed upon and unambiguous.

Many times, however, care for one reason or another cannot be delivered at home, and some other institution is required, such as a hospice facility or a nursing home. If the patient has been transferred to a hospice residential facility, there is no problem outlining and sticking to a plan of comfort care only; hospice workers are clearly and expertly trained in these matters. A nursing home may be a problem, however. Here there are many more people involved in giving care, and at each shift change, the staff needs to be instructed. The nursing director, the nurse in charge of each shift, other staff nurses or aides who will be interacting with the patient must all be informed and educated about the goals.

This difficulty is further compounded when it is necessary to have the patient hospitalized for symptom relief. Here the number of caregivers is far higher, and new doctors enter the picture, which can lead to undesired results. This was underscored for me a few years ago when the first turning point to comfort care was taken too late.

Upstairs in the bedroom of her vacation cottage, Nancy heard a loud explosion from below. Racing down to the first floor, she saw her husband Stephen staggering up the stairs from the basement with his clothes ablaze. Stephen had gone to the basement to relight the pilot of the hot water heater. Racing back to the bedroom, Nancy grabbed a bedspread, threw it around Stephen, and rolled him onto the floor to put out the flames. Stephen's nylon jacket had melted across his back, and his hands, face, and neck were badly burned.

"Shut off the gas!" Stephen managed to blurt out despite his excruciating pain. As Nancy did this, she saw that one of the joists in the basement had caught fire. She was able to put the fire out with an extinguisher that was fortunately nearby.

Stephen needed help and right away. Nancy ran to the phone only to find that it was dead. Later, they discovered the telephone wire had been burned through. This was 1978, before the era of cell phones, and Nancy's only option was to leave Stephen and drive to the neighbor's house for help. Luckily they were home.

As the emergency unfolded, I was notified of the accident since both Stephen and Nancy were my patients. I left the office immediately and met them at the local hospital. At about the same time, word reached Stephen and Nancy's grown daughter, Susan. In her late twenties, Susan was married and raising children of her own. In addition to her parents, I knew Susan very well, too. On hearing the news of her father's accident, Susan also headed for the hospital.

We all arrived simultaneously at the emergency room of the local hospital. The emergency room doctors quickly determined that Stephen had third-degree burns over large areas of his body. Everyone recognized that his injuries were too severe for the capabilities of the local hospital so Stephen was immediately transferred to one of the teaching hospitals in Boston twenty miles away, where he would receive the best, latest, and most sophisticated care possible in their intensive care burn unit. Stephen, in his seventies, was a retired tree surgeon and still remarkably fit physically, and it seemed clear to all that everything possible should be done to try to help him recover from this terrible injury.

Some twenty-four years later while writing this book, I interviewed Susan in the backyard of her home. Together, we reflected on what happened to her father during six months of intensive care treatment. Stephen was obviously very sick when he arrived in the burn unit, but Susan remembered that initially he was talking coherently. Describing her father's arrival, Susan said: "Initially he seemed in fairly good shape. He was able to joke with the nurses, 'If I had known you weren't going to give me lunch, I would have brought a sandwich.'"

"That burn unit was incredible. All they do for those patients!" Susan recalled that the doctor in charge was at the top of his field, providing the most advanced approaches to burn care. The resources available to her father were great in depth and sophistication, representing truly the very best care that could be found anywhere. The burn unit team brought all their expertise to bear with multiple surgical procedures over many weeks to try to repair Stephen's massive physical injuries. The procedures included surgical removal of burned tissue, and skin grafts to cover the third-degree burns of his hands, face, neck, and back. He received meticulous care to control the ever present susceptibility to infection, intravenous feedings with special nutrients, and a panoply of supportive measures. The doctors were hopeful that Stephen could be restored to a reasonably normal state so their efforts were maximal in every way. The family was awed by and grateful for all the doctors were doing. As Stephen's primary care doctor, I recall feeling the same way.

Unfortunately, Stephen's initial responsiveness did not last long. Within two days after admission, Susan remembered, "He did not talk much anymore, and all he would do was look around. The last thing he said to us was on the second day there. 'That Jell-O didn't taste very good.'"

Stephen's initial skin grafts had some success, but they never were successful on his back; he began to have a series of complications. He developed pneumonia, not an unusual thing in critically ill patients. During the second anesthesia in the operating room, as the doctors pursued the grafting attempts, Stephen had a cardiac arrest from which he was resuscitated. "After the cardiac arrest, he became less and less responsive. The doctors said he had had oxygen loss to the brain." The explosion in which Stephen was burned had occurred in May, but by now the days had led into weeks, and the weeks into months. The summer came and went.

Eventually, Stephen's kidneys began to fail. He was appearing less and less likely to survive the ordeal, and, even if he did, he probably wouldn't regain any sort of productive life. "In June and July we were still hopeful, but by August we no longer had hope. Still, the doctors wanted to operate more." Susan and Nancy began to feel the first stirrings of misgiving.

"My father was a very active man, very energetic. We wondered if he would ever be able to talk again, but the doctors said they did not know. What loomed ahead didn't seem to be the kind of life he would want. He had been adamant about the living will, which both he and my mother had signed. It said clearly he didn't want what seemed to be happening to him. He and my mother were proud of having living wills. In those days, not many people had them. Over the course of several weeks, my mother began reminding the doctors of my father's living will, saying that he didn't want his life prolonged senselessly. But each time the doctors said 'All hope is not gone, not yet.'"

"It was a fight, to let him have some peace. My mother said it was the hardest thing she ever did in life, to get the doctors to follow his living will."

During another trip to the operating room for further surgery under anesthesia, Stephen had a second cardiac arrest. After that he was on a pulmonary resuscitator that breathed for him with a tube into his trachea. Stephen had a tube through the abdominal wall into his stomach, through which he received liquid food and nutrients. He had a tube into the bladder to drain his urine so his bladder would not become distended. And there were intravenous lines in place for fluids and various medications. Stephen's liver function by now had also deteriorated. His bone marrow production of blood cells was failing, and he became anemic. Mentally, Stephen was essentially nonresponsive.

Nancy's upset and anger gradually grew as the hopelessness of the situation became more evident. Acutely aware of the situation, I asked Nancy and Susan to come into my medical office in Concord, Massachusetts, to discuss what could be done. They readily agreed.

I told them I thought the burn team had become so emotionally invested in Stephen's treatment that they were unable to see how poor his prospects were. Bent on rescuing Stephen, the team was unable to allow him to die in peace. Nancy and Susan completely agreed. This was 1978 when few doctors recognized that there are situations in which the patient is better served by pulling back heroic restorative efforts and turning one's energies, instead, to shepherding the patient through the dying process with comfort care only.

I telephoned the hospital physician leading Stephen's team and told him our conclusions. "The best way out of the situation," I suggested as tactfully as I could, "might be to transfer Stephen back to my care at our community hospital, where I could allow him to die with comfort care measures only." There was an uncomfortably long silence on the phone. It probably only lasted ten or fifteen seconds, but it seemed an eternity.

Finally the physician on the other end said in a subdued voice, "I think you're right. I'll arrange to transfer him."

The next day, Stephen was brought by ambulance to our community hospital in Concord. Years later, as Susan and I reminisced, she told me of his leaving the burn unit. "The nurses were preparing him for transfer. One of them leaned over and gave him a kiss. She said, 'Stephen, you are going home to Concord.' He then amazed us by clearly saying, 'Thank you very much.' We could not believe it, but three people heard him." Stephen had said nothing for months, but clearly must have had some degree of awareness.

I briefed the nurses at the hospital in Concord ahead of time so there was a clear-cut understanding of our plan and responsibility—to allow Stephen to die without any further distress. All tubes were removed other than his bladder catheter (for comfort), and all medications were stopped other than morphine, which we used in liberal doses to control restlessness and pain. Stephen was unresponsive and remained so until he died two days later, on May 28—six months after he had been admitted to intensive care. His family remained at his bedside, and they were grateful that the ordeal was over. It was an abrupt ending to months of aggressive care, but the family and I were certain we had done the right thing. Relief was an important feeling in us all.

My phone call to the doctor treating Stephen at the burn unit marked the first turning point in his dying, the point at which the goal of the treatment changed from heroic efforts to restore his health to shepherding him through the dying process. In this instance, the change in treatment goals came too far down the intensive care road. Looking at things retrospectively years later, the turning point should have come much earlier. But this was more than two decades ago, and relentless intensive treatment was the norm then. Now, we would have addressed whether or not Stephen had reached the first turning point in a formal way at a much earlier point in his final illness. We would have found the probabilities of his recovering a reasonable life too small and would have made the decision to withdraw aggressive treatment weeks earlier, and a new, more appropriate setting for care would have been chosen.

Looking back on her father's turning point, Susan says, "If you know what you believe in, you have to stand up for it." Asked if she had the experience to live over again, what she would have done differently, Susan reflected, "I would have insisted on better communication with the doctors caring for him." Stephen's case was for all of us a learning experience in the days in which end-of-life care was beginning to change in many ways, and for me personally it clearly marked a change in how I looked at the problems of hopelessly ill patients.

The setting in which end-of-life care is rendered influences not only the degree to which the patient and family can maintain control, it also influences the quality of comfort care the patient receives. A study from Brown Medical School in 2004 indicated that care at home or in a hospice setting was more likely to be of higher quality with respect to "symptom amelioration, physician communication, emotional support, and being treated with respect."[4] All of these aspects of comfort care were of lower quality in patients who died in institutions.

Elizabeth's story illustrates a death that occurred in the appropriate and best setting after the turning point to comfort care was properly recognized and implemented.

Elizabeth, a patient of mine, was a gracious, elegant woman who had raised two daughters with her husband, Robert, a schoolteacher. In her early fifties, Elizabeth was diagnosed with ovarian cancer. She first had surgery to remove as much of the tumor as possible, but, because the cancer had spread to her pelvis and abdomen, it could not be removed completely without damaging vital organs. During the following year, she had chemotherapy given in pulses of treatment every few weeks. After each bout of chemotherapy, Elizabeth had nausea, vomiting, and an increase in her overall distress. With time, even between chemotherapy sessions, she had increased abdominal pain and general weakness.

Elizabeth put up a valiant fight. As her condition worsened because of the advancing cancer and the side effects of chemotherapy, she eventually became housebound. Still, she pushed herself to make the burdensome trips to see the oncologist. Robert and their daughters also encouraged Elizabeth to keep up the fight: to get out of bed every day, drink and eat to maintain her strength, and walk regularly so that she did not become moribund.

Eventually, it became apparent that Elizabeth's cancer was aggressive and overtaking her despite everything she and we did. In my regular house calls, I could see that Elizabeth was exhausted. She no longer had the energy to get out of bed, eat, or walk. Tension was developing within the family as her husband and daughters tried to do what they thought was best—pushing her to do activities that she no longer had the energy for. Her devoted family feared they were "failing" as they watched Elizabeth lose weight and require larger doses of morphine for abdominal pain.

One day I decided to intervene and said to Elizabeth in a gentle but direct way, "It seems to me that you, your family, and the oncologist are doing everything humanly possible, but the cancer is unstoppable."

"I'm exhausted," said Elizabeth. "I can't push myself any further. I can't go on."

In these situations, I think it is usually possible to deliver comforting news along with the bad: "We can make you very comfortable. We can arrange hospice care here in your home. You could have intravenous morphine that can be dialed up at will for pain relief."

"I'd like that," said Elizabeth with obvious relief. "I'd like that very much. I just want to die in peace."

Over the course of the next few days, I had several conversations with Elizabeth, Robert, and their two grown daughters at Elizabeth's bedside. (It is important not to have these conversations "behind the patient's back," but instead with all family members together, including the patient if he or she is able to participate in medical decision making.) Elizabeth made it clear that she felt further efforts to stop the cancer did not have a high enough chance of success to be worth the price she was paying in side effects. After the initial shock, everyone in the family embraced the idea of taking the turning point, of switching the focus of Elizabeth's treatment from attempts to fight the cancer to comfort care to ease her dying process in the simplest setting possible—her home.

Robert and Elizabeth's daughters were supportive of her wishes and wholly committed to caring for her at home. They set to work turning the dining room into a downstairs bedroom for Elizabeth. All of the dining room furniture was moved out and a hospital bed was moved in, along with many of Elizabeth's personal effects and favorite pieces of furniture.

Hospice was engaged. Hospice workers have immeasurable experience ministering to the physical and psychological needs of dying patients and their families, and they were a big help to us. Hospice is committed neither to hastening death nor prolonging dying. Their workers enter the scene when the prognosis has become hopeless, and the patient is clearly dying. They have tremendous expertise in pain management, and they were immediately helpful in supervising the intravenous line that had been put in place for administering morphine.

As Elizabeth's primary care doctor, I took over her care from her oncologist. I visited her regularly and worked closely with the nurses who saw her daily and with the hospice personnel. Elizabeth and her family learned how to control the steady infusion of morphine to keep her pain free. Robert and her daughters stopped urging Elizabeth to pursue activities like eating, drinking, and moving about, which she no longer wanted to do. Everyone accepted the inevitability of Elizabeth's approaching death. We were at ease because, at the turning point, all had agreed upon a redefinition of the goal of Elizabeth's care. No one was striving any longer for the unlikely or the impossible.

I explained to the family that Elizabeth's lack of interest in food or drink was a normal part of the dying process. So, too, was her somnolence and diminished responsiveness with the increasing doses of morphine. When Elizabeth was alert enough to converse, there would often be comforting reminiscences of times past and reassurances about what the family would do when she died. Although Robert and their daughters were immensely sad to watch Elizabeth slipping away, they valued the peacefulness that came over her with the change in treatment focus.

Toward the end, I visited more frequently to remind the family that they were doing the right thing and to assure Elizabeth that I would be there for her regularly to help with whatever came up. What families need at these times are support and reassurance and, especially, recognition of the pain *they* are suffering and the selflessness of their efforts on behalf of their dying loved one.

Elizabeth died peacefully in her home, surrounded by her family, three weeks after taking the turning point. Her death was in many ways the ideal in these circumstances. Her family was satisfied that they had done the right thing and were happy that they had participated in her dying at home. Most importantly, Elizabeth, her family, the nurses, the hospice personnel, and I—all of us—regarded her dying not as a failure to stop her cancer but as a success in shepherding her through the dying process with the least distress and most peacefulness possible. Most of us would prefer to be Elizabeth dying peacefully at home surrounded by family rather than my mother, Richard, or Stephen who were trapped in medical futility.

Morphine was a godsend to Elizabeth and is an age-old remedy used by doctors to ease death. In her case, the morphine probably did hasten her death by hours or days, but this consequence was acceptable to everyone concerned because it gave Elizabeth the pain relief she needed. (The issue of an earlier death in patients receiving large doses of morphine is discussed in detail in succeeding chapters.)

The bottom line is that end-of-life care is generally better when the patient is in a simple setting. We need to educate all caregivers—at home or in a nursing home—that death is expected to take place in such a setting and that transferring a patient to the hospital is not an option except under very special circumstances, such as to control unrelieved, intolerable symptoms. These exceptions should occur only when palliative services cannot be delivered in a simpler setting; in such cases, the warmth and intimacy of the patient's home environment is sacrificed for technical expertise—a trade-off that sometimes is unavoidable. There are hospitals and nursing homes that have settings for dying that approach the peacefulness of a patient's home, but they are rare. When these high-tech but peaceful settings exist, they are likely to be hospice-run.

Talk with your physician to find the setting that most closely meets your needs. Most people prefer to be at home, but that may involve family who are unable or not skilled enough to help. In that case, supplementary, skilled home care can be arranged through local social services or a nursing agency, as well as hospice. Staying at home successfully almost always involves getting sufficient help from these community services.

Some hospice programs involve a physical place to which the patient may be transferred, but many programs operate almost entirely within the patient's home. Initially, they will evaluate the patient's needs and then set up a plan that draws from their store of services: nurses, aides, pain control technicians, doctors, and social workers. If they do not have the in-house expertise, they will help to arrange for it and to supervise and integrate services.

When asked to join in the care of a patient, hospice can provide a tremendous amount, but none of this conflicts with other consultants or programs that might already be operating. If a practical nurse or other aide is necessary around the clock in the home, hospice will integrate their services into the overall picture. In all of my experience with hospice, I never stopped being the provider in charge, but hospice joined the effort as colleagues with a common goal. As you can tell, I am an advocate of the hospice movement.

Patients and families sometimes comment that if hospice is called, then all hope must be gone and the end must be close; they don't want to make that admission. In practice, however, when hospice enters the situation, almost always there is a decrease in anxiety and an increase in comfort for the patient and the family. If health providers do not suggest a hospice referral when dying seems less than six months away, you should bring it up. There is further information about hospice in Appendix A.

Where to give comfort care is often a complex decision. The family and patient advocates need to ask, carefully, questions about what services are necessary, who can successfully deliver them in what setting, where the most control over the desired manner of dying can be exerted, and which setting will provide the most comfort and emotional support for the patient. This should be a formal discussion with the physician and is best done well ahead of time, when possible.

Probability, Certainty, and Medical Futility: Important Considerations in Comfort Care

The stories told in this chapter about Marie, my brother Bob, and Stephen address how the decision to render comfort care only was arrived at, and in each instance, questions of probability and medical futility were in the background as these decisions were made. Sometimes, it is clear that restoration of health is not possible, and this helps the patient and family to take the turning point. At other times, however, there is still some possibility of improvement, and the question then becomes how likely that possibility is.

The decision to make one more effort to restore a degree of health depends on the likelihood that the course being contemplated will have at least some success—that the effort and side effects will be worth it. How strong must the probability be to justify undertaking the action? There are many who would say that any chance of improvement is worth shooting for, while others would maintain they need a high probability of success before they are willing to undertake further treatment with side effects. And there are many variations in between. The basic personality of the individual and his or her approach to life certainly influences this decision.

How much suffering is likely to be incurred as a result of any new treatment is also a major factor. If the proposed treatment has little in the way of side effects and is relatively easy to initiate, then the patient may want to elect it even though the probability of its helping is low. On the other hand, if a treatment has considerable side effects, the patient may be reluctant to undertake it even though the probability of helping is moderate. It all depends on the individual and the circumstances.

In all cases, the most important thing is to address the options in a formal, deliberate meeting and discuss them in light of all available evidence and with all persons able to help the patient in the decision. Once a formal decision-making process has been undertaken, the appropriate choice usually emerges. This choice then be acknowledged by all, and the treatment goals modified accordingly.

The physician should give his or her best estimate as to the likelihood of treatment success and the downside of undesired effects. If he or she is not forthcoming with this information, you should press for an opinion, including substantiating evidence. The physician should always go through the exercise of explaining what he or she would do, while emphasizing that the final decision belongs to you. Then, you can take the physician's opinion as another bit of evidence in making your own decision.

Certainty is always desired in medical decision making but seldom achieved in practice. The higher your need for certainty, the more difficult the outcome may be to achieve. To be very certain, you need a greater number of tests, interventions, and procedures, and this has its own very real price. At some point, you will have to forgo the need for high certainty and accept reasonable probability.

If you and your family carefully and formally consider probabilities and the degree of probability with which you are comfortable, then it is unlikely that your actions will degenerate into medical futility. This is the worst situation of all—when a patient pushes on with (or the family encourages) measures that are unlikely to help and at the same time cause further suffering. Doctors are increasingly and properly resisting the occasional demands from patients and families for continuation of medical care that seems to the caregivers to be futile. The Code of Medical Ethics of the American Medical Association, 1996–97, states: "Physicians are not ethically obligated to deliver care that, in their best professional judgment, will not have a reasonable chance of benefiting their patients. Patients should not be given treatments simply because they demand them." (This does not mean that a young person determined to live who pushes for an experimental treatment is necessarily engaging in pursuit of futility. The point is that when there is *no* reasonable expectation of a good result, treatments aimed at cure or reversal of the process become futile.)

Careful and detailed communication among patients, families, and physicians—and the reliance on the degree of probability with which the patient is comfortable—will in most instances prevent the patient from going down a destructive and burdensome path of futility and will help ensure that decisions at the first turning point are thoughtfully made.

4

Pain Control

❧

Control of Pain, a Critical Issue

Pain is often a symptom during the dying process, particularly in patients with cancer who have metastatic disease. Although some patients die without any pain at all, when pain does occur, failure to control it properly can be extremely debilitating and demoralizing. Pain control is essential to a peaceful death.

In recent decades, the medical profession has made great strides in controlling pain, such that it is now rare that patients have unrelieved pain. New medications, new and better ways of delivering medication, surgical procedures that sometimes can interrupt pain pathways or relieve the basic cause of the pain, the use of radiation for pain coming from metastatic cancer, and other measures are being used aggressively for comfort care. Doctors now consider pain control a medical subspecialty, and there are doctors and clinics devoting their entire efforts to this subject. When the primary care physician is not successful in controlling pain, he or she can consult specialists who are experts in pain control.

In spite of these tremendous improvements, more than one recent study has shown that patients still may not have their pain properly and sufficiently relieved. Patients and their families must discuss this matter with their physicians and not settle for getting by with partial pain relief—it needs to be *good* pain relief.

Pain Relievers in Sufficient Doses

The first step in prescribing pain relief is to decide which category of medication is needed. Minimal pain is usually controlled with ordinary medications, and the very simplest (aspirin, acetaminophen [Tylenol], ibuprofen [Motrin or Advil], and other similar over-the-counter drugs) may be all that is necessary. We are all familiar with using these for mild pain—they do a good job. Moderate pain can be controlled with prescription medicines in the codeine category, but more severe or unrelieved pain requires the use of the major pain relievers (morphine being the most widely used example).

Heroin (diamorphine) deserves a special comment as a possible alternative to morphine since it can be used as a cancer drug. Heroin is clearly a major and potent pain reliever, but its abuse and availability for street sale have so far made it unacceptable for legal medical use in the United States and Canada. However, it is the major analgesic of choice in many hospices in other countries. One advantage of heroin is that it is more soluble than morphine, allowing smaller injected volumes—a consideration when large doses are necessary for pain control.[1] In spite of this advantage, there is no evidence of clear-cut, overriding superiority of heroin compared to morphine, and I do not feel patients in this country are at an overall disadvantage because of its unavailability.[2]

The proper dose of any analgesic necessary for major pain is the amount necessary to relieve pain, and at the end of life there is no maximum amount beyond which the doctor should not go. If life is shortened by the necessary use of high doses of drugs, such as morphine, then it is acceptable legally and ethically since the goal is to relieve suffering. This is well known in medicine as the "double effect." The most common error made in pain control is to use insufficiently powerful drugs in insufficient doses. Both the amount per dose and the frequency of dosing should be increased until the patient is relieved of pain, and this includes advancing to continuous intravenous administration of the medicine when necessary.

Using the right pain medication in the right dose is unfortunately something that is not consistently done for patients suffering at the end of life. Some physicians continue to be hampered by old concepts of what the proper potency and dose of pain medication should be. They may continue to have unjustified fears of using too much medication and thereby depressing respirations. Nurses may have concerns about addiction or dosage levels that are unsubstantiated, and pharmacists may be too cautious in their advice. If you believe any of this is true in your situation, you should first speak directly with your doctor, and, if your concerns and needs are not met, ask for a consultation from a pain control expert. This is clearly your right as a patient, family member, or designated agent. If you are still not helped sufficiently, Compassion and Choices (see Appendix D) has a patient advocacy unit that will help you address such problems, and they are only a telephone call away.

STAYING AHEAD OF PAIN

The patient with chronic pain is best treated when medication is used in a way that allows the patient to stay ahead of the pain. It is important to use enough medication in a continuous way so that pain is not allowed to break through the medicine being used. (Pain is harder to control when it is not *steadily* controlled.) Peaks and valleys of pain and pain medicine levels should be avoided, and a comfortable steady state is the desired goal, no matter which category of drug is being used.

With severe pain and the use of the major morphine-like medications, the patient and family should have the on-the-spot authority and necessary instruction to increase the dose and/or frequency when pain is insufficiently controlled. They should not have to wait for the doctor to be contacted and "permission" to be granted. If the physician gives parameters within which the patient may adjust the dose, the patient has a sense of control over the situation. If the ability to increase pain medication as needed is not under the control of the patient and/or family, anxiety, agitation, and frustration rise markedly.

Ask your doctor about long-acting oral forms of the major narcotics that are excellent in preventing peaks and valleys when taken on a regular schedule. In addition, pumps are now available that can deliver medication at a prescribed rate beneath the skin in a continuous fashion, probably the best way to avoid the peaks and valleys. Home care agencies and hospice can set these pumps up and provide strong support for the patient and family using them. For truly major pain, this has been a boon.

ADDICTION AT THE END OF LIFE: NOT A PROBLEM

Addiction to morphine and other major painkillers is often in people's minds as a problem when large and/or repeated doses are used. This is not a valid concern for patients with major pain, particularly when a person in pain near the end of life is likely to need continuous medication until death occurs. Addiction is simply not an issue in this circumstance. The dying patient should continue to receive pain medication in whatever doses and for whatever length of time is necessary—to the end. Increasing doses may be needed to effect the desired relief as time goes by, due to the development of tolerance to the medication, but that is expected. Too often we confuse this situation with the problems of addicts who use street drugs to seek a high, not relief of severe pain. That is substance abuse, a matter of great concern, but the dying person need not think about this. Confusing these two issues has unfortunately resulted in reduced availability for dying patients of some very good pain relievers, such as OxyContin. Also, pharmacists have become wary of stocking medications that are popularly abused, because they fear being robbed by criminals who wish to sell the drugs on the street. This occasionally makes it more difficult for end-of-life patients to meet their legitimate needs.

SIDE EFFECTS OF PAIN RELIEVERS

Most pain medications have some side effects, and it is important for the patient and family to know about them and how to cope with them. The minor pain relievers (over-the-counter medications, such as aspirin, acetaminophen, and ibuprofen), have few side effects, although some can produce stomach inflammation that is symptomatic—heartburn, nausea, and sometimes actual stomach pain. Prolonged use of these common pain relievers can produce enough stomach irritation that bleeding results, which is a major complication. However, simply taking these less powerful drugs with food usually prevents troubles.

The codeine category drugs (codeine, Percocet, Percodan, and the like) can be more of a problem. They frequently produce nausea and constipation. Nausea may be prevented simply by taking it with food or in a smaller dose, and the constipation usually responds to simple measures, such as milk of magnesia, prunes, or bran cereal. Occasionally, these mid-category drugs can result in excessive somnolence or a spaced-out, unpleasant feeling.

The morphine-like medications (morphine in various forms, Demerol, Dilaudid, etc.) may produce all of the previous side effects, but in addition may bring on hallucinations and psychological disturbances. In big doses, these drugs may produce somnolence, the severity of which depends on the dose, and respirations may be slowed to the point that dying occurs sooner than it would have were the morphine not used (not necessarily a bad thing, as we have discussed elsewhere in the book). The bottom line, however, is that the physician should be able to guide the patient through these various side effects, either changing the dose or mode and frequency of administration, using some other medication to counteract side effects, or utilizing a completely different drug that can give the same desired effects without the undesired side effects. Pain specialists and hospice workers are particularly adept in helping in this way.

Although detailed information on whatever drug a patient is using is usually supplied by the physician or pharmacist, sometimes people wish to pursue information on their own, either on the Internet or in various compendia of drug information. A reliable description of drugs and their side effects can be found in the *Physicians' Desk Reference*, an annually updated book that is in most libraries and easily accessible. In my experience, I always felt that it was a great benefit when a patient or family took the time to become fully informed on the medications they use. (Too often patients don't even know the names of what they are taking, much less the purpose and side effects.)

5

WHAT YOU SHOULD EXPECT FROM YOUR DOCTORS AND NURSES

Most patients and families want the physician to play a central role in end-of-life care. This chapter is intended to familiarize patients and families with what to expect of their physician in this respect and suggests some specific questions to ask.

HISTORICAL CONSTRAINTS ON DOCTORS

Be aware that doctors may be driven by traditional styles of practicing medicine, which can stand in the way of modern approaches to end-of-life care. When considering your expectations of what your doctor should be able to do for you, keep the following in mind.

First, watch out for a paternalistic approach that often characterized medical decision making in the past. Back then, the doctor's word was law, and he simply told the patient and family what to do. His pronouncement was usually accepted without dissent, and patients ceded their rights to the physician and the system. In recent decades, this approach has been replaced by shared decision making in which patients' and families' wishes are regarded as highly important to patient care. This is a tremendous improvement, but unfortunately there are still instances in which the patient and family are not properly involved in charting the course of treatment—a holdover from the past.

Second, the Hippocratic oath has for generations caused physicians to mishandle one of the most important aspects of patient care—the treatment of pain. The oath was interpreted to admonish physicians never to cause harm by giving too much pain medication. This meant that many patients had far too little. Modern interpretation of the Hippocratic oath, however, has been slowly changing through a difficult process of education. Physicians have realized that sometimes very large doses of pain medication need to be utilized in order to control intolerable pain—doses that can depress respirations, such that life is shortened by hours or a few days.

Flora was a patient of mine years ago who had metastatic breast cancer that had spread to the bone. This was in the early days of chemotherapy, when we did not have very good ways of dealing with recurrent disease. Surgery, radiation, and attempts at chemotherapy had failed. No other treatment had any prospect of significantly changing the course of the disease, and comfort care was left as the only reasonable choice.

Unfortunately, the amounts of morphine necessary to control pain (by then severe) kept escalating. I felt we needed to give more, but my medical and surgical colleagues, who were participating in her care, felt that it would be too dangerous. "We might cause the patient to have depressed respirations that would shorten life, or she might become addicted." I gave in and stayed with "safe" amounts of morphine. I was not experienced enough then to defy advice from older colleagues, although I do remember feeling terribly upset that we were not controlling Flora's pain. We clearly undertreated her.

I am sure there were others who also had insufficiently treated pain, but Flora stands out in my mind to this day as having suffered through a bad death. The Hippocratic oath, strictly interpreted, had won out, and the patient had lost. To this day I have persistent regret about how she was handled. It was a defining time in my career, and I wish somehow Flora could know that—but at the time we just didn't know any better. Fortunately, this is something that now happens much less frequently. We have learned a lot about pain management. The amount of medication necessary for the welfare of the patient has become the guiding principle.

The third constraining historical point that has stood in the way of proper comfort care is that, until the past couple of decades, students in medical school and young doctors in training programs were taught for the most part to strive always to try to cure patients. Comfort care only was not seen as a valid medical decision. Fortunately, this also has changed, and students and residents are now being taught comfort care as a defined strategy in end-of-life management.

With these thoughts in mind, what can you reasonably expect from your doctors?

QUESTIONS TO ASK

If you have been diagnosed with a serious, life-threatening illness, here are some questions you would do well to ask your doctor at the outset. They may help to organize your thinking about what is ahead, how you will cope with the future, and how helpful your doctor will or will not be once the goal of treatment changes to comfort care only.

What is the nature of my illness, my prognosis, and my life expectancy?

Your physician should be proactive in initiating discussions about the dying process and what it entails for the individual patient so that you are fully informed and supported. You may not feel comfortable bringing up subjects related to dying and end-of-life care, so the physician *should* take the lead in discussing the problems. If not, you should bring it up. The patient and family need to do their part to open the doors to frank exchanges of information and thoughts with their doctor, even if it is not forthcoming. Good communication is the responsibility of both sides, and once the subjects are initially broached, they are then much more easily discussed.

You should expect your doctor to give you the facts. There are a few people who prefer not to know the details of their illness, but most of us do. It is much easier to cope with things when you know the facts. From the physician's point of view, I have found that it is much easier for the doctor to advise and deal with a patient who is totally informed. It may be difficult at the outset, but getting the facts straight will help in the long run.

All options for treatment and symptom alleviation need to be explained to you along with side effects, risks, financial costs, and probabilities of success, and the prognosis must be made clear. This needs to be a very straightforward discussion that is direct *and understood*. You need truly to understand your options, and the doctor also needs to be satisfied that you understand. Two examples of wives not being psychologically prepared for the death of their husbands indicate how upsetting the lack of factual understanding can be.

The first instance occurred in the emergency room of a community hospital. I was the internist on call for the weekend when an elderly man vomiting blood came in with his distraught wife. I had never seen him before, and his own doctors were in another nearby community. Nevertheless, it was clear he had terminal cancer of the esophagus, and, to me, the acute and profuse bleeding seemed to be a relatively easy way for him to die. We were not going to be able to stop the bleeding. He was already in shock and poorly responsive but not suffering. However, his wife was astounded and emotionally crushed when I told her he was close to dying. She was totally unprepared for this. It was clear that he, too, had not come to grips with the situation and had not said his goodbyes to his wife. In order to give them time to understand what was happening, I transfused him with three pints of blood, giving them a few more hours. It was incredibly upsetting for the wife and the patient alike.

The second instance was a couple who were patients of one of my medical colleagues. I knew the wife as a casual friend, and her husband had terminal cancer. On Friday afternoon her husband's physician and I discussed the likelihood that he would die over the weekend from his disease so I made an elective house call that night to get thoroughly acquainted with the current situation and to be better able to care for him in his dying moments. After I had examined him, I asked his wife to tell me what she had learned from my colleague about her husband's condition. She was oblivious to his pending death and was appalled at the fact he might die that weekend. I had to spend two hours that evening bringing her up to speed with events. I am convinced her own doctor had told her, but like so many people in that situation, she had not heard him. It was a failure of communication.

Will you interpret for me what other specialists advise?

This is part of being informed about the facts. You need to understand what the various doctors on your team are thinking and proposing. Ask your family doctor to translate their advice into language you understand. Your doctor needs to be the interface between you and the various specialists who may be participating in your care. All decisions about your care should come through your family doctor so that there is one leader to whom you and your family may turn. This is as true for comfort care as it was for earlier phases of aggressive attempts to improve or cure.

Patients are often bewildered by the complexities of the health care system, and they need a clear-cut leader and interpreter. A physician who is a decisive leader is not reverting to paternalism. (Atul Gawande, a younger doctor who recently went through his medical training at one of the teaching centers in Boston, wondered whether doctors should be more forceful in advising patients about what is the best path for them to take in problem situations. He said, "[As] the field grows ever more complex and technological, the real task isn't to banish paternalism; the real task is to preserve kindness.")[1]

Will you be there for me? Will you continue to play a leading role in my care no matter what the setting (home, hospice facility, nursing home, hospital)?

This is an important thing to expect from your doctor—the assurance that he or she will be there for you. It is important to bring this up as early as possible. Fear of abandonment is a common feeling in dying persons. What a patient needs to hear is, "You won't be alone. I'll be here often and whenever needed." As a person approaches dying, physician presence is psychologically essential. Even when there is no real change in the needs of the patient, a regular visit by the doctor is calming.

This fear of abandonment can be very real as patients are referred by the attending physician to other doctors who may take over a large segment of the patient's care because of their specialty status (such as the oncologist), or as patients are referred to nursing homes, hospice units, the visiting nurse association, and various other community agencies. "Strangers" may begin to take over their care. "Where is my doctor? I don't see him anymore!" No matter how good hospice workers or other specialists are, they begin as strangers, and this can feel like abandonment. The patient and the doctor need to talk about this very early in the illness and be clear about the doctor's role.

The physician should not tend to withdraw as death approaches. Unfortunately, this does occur at times, not as an overt rejection of the patient and the situation, but rather a handing off of responsibility to nurses, hospice, or other caregivers as the challenges of trying to restore health wane. The subconscious feeling by the physician may be that now others can handle the situation for most problems that arise in comfort care, but this is not the case. Not only does the physician have the best expertise to cope with the various symptoms of dying, but psychologically his or her continued and frequent presence is invaluable in making the patient feel as peaceful as possible. The laying on of hands and understanding support by the physician continues to be an essential ingredient of successful end-of-life care.

I had a wonderful friend, John, who lived not far from me and who never consulted doctors. In his early seventies, he developed bladder outlet obstruction due to prostate cancer. He had increasing trouble passing his urine and realized he had to have the help of a physician, so he asked me to be his doctor. I was honored to be asked and agreed readily. Unfortunately, his cancer was far advanced, and there were few options for treatment.

John was a man who was fascinated by how things worked, so when I gave him hormone treatment for his prostate cancer (the only feasible option), temporarily relieving his bladder outlet obstruction, he was profoundly grateful. For a few months, the hormones shrank the prostate cancer, and he was able to urinate almost normally. One day as I was passing his house in my automobile, he saw me and hailed me down. He told me to get out of the car, at which point he thanked me profusely and kissed me on both cheeks in the middle of the road.

Unfortunately, when the temporary effect of the hormone treatment wore off, we had no further treatment to offer other than comfort care. Just as these things were happening, I quit my private practice after almost thirty years to move to another job within the profession. I hated to leave John in his terminal illness, but I arranged for a colleague to assume his care, someone I thought would do a good job, and I assured John that I would continue to follow his situation as a friend. As it turned out, however, the new doctor did not make house calls and also tended to delegate his responsibilities to the home care nurse. As a result, as John needed more medical attention, he continued to call me for help. I would go to his home, assess what was going on, and then telephone the new doctor to suggest some move. The other physician was always glad to get a suggestion and would almost always implement it—but he never himself came to the bedside to give the patient the feeling that he, the doctor, was there for John, the patient. This distressed me a great deal, so I continued to follow the patient closely until the time of his death at home. I did not do anything curative, but I let him know a doctor cared and was trying to make him more comfortable. That alone was sufficient to make his death somewhat more peaceful.

A physician has a tremendous responsibility to make patients feel that they are cared for in the best way possible, which at the end of life means making them as comfortable as possible psychologically, looking after the details of physical comfort and pain relief, and in general following them closely and personally with compassion for their plight. Above all, a physician must not allow patients to feel a lack of full attention and support. Without that support, suffering is always magnified.

You need to have a doctor who will honor these responsibilities. If you do not, try to do something about it. Either get your doctor to understand your needs by direct discussion, or, if this does not work, ask for a referral to another doctor. You can also ask other doctor friends you may have, talk with other specialists you may have met during your illness, talk with the local hospice or hospital officials, consult the local district medical society, or ask a medical social worker.

Will you respect my wishes as expressed in my living will, and ask others to do the same?

Not making sure of this point was the big mistake I made in the case of my mother's doctor and the pacemaker decision. Don't neglect to ask this in a point-blank manner.

The physician must make every reasonable effort to comply with the wishes of a patient's advance directive (or with the instructions of a properly designated health care agent if the patient is not competent to participate in medical decision making). If the doctor is unable to do so because of personal beliefs, the doctor has the responsibility to assist the patient in finding a physician who will do so.

Will you communicate freely about my problems with my family and me?

Sometimes, patients do not want anyone to know details of their difficulties, even family, but most of us would like our families informed in appropriate detail. It is wise to ask your doctor about doing this and, at the same time, to give permission for it to be done and with which persons you designate. Be specific. If there is only one person whom you want to be your spokesperson, let the doctor know. This will preserve your privacy and also will keep your doctor from being besieged with numerous contacts from family members.

If the patient is able to communicate and understand, conversations between the doctor and the family should generally be held in the presence of the patient, which will reduce any sense of isolation felt by the patient. This is not always advisable, but most of the time it is.

What is your opinion of the best course?

I believe physicians should commit themselves as to what they think is the wisest course. Too often the doctor will present all the options (which is necessary and proper), but will not follow this up with a clear indication of which course of action in his or her opinion is best under the circumstances. It is not fair to patients to outline all the various options and then say "it is up to you." Patients do make the final decision, but as part of deciding, they need to know what the doctor thinks is best. At times, the choices are 50/50 in terms of desirability, and the doctor can make this clear.

Will you help if there is a disagreement among family or consultants regarding the best course of action?

In interpreting the medical situation and the options open to you, your physician has a particularly important (and difficult) role to play when there is a disagreement among family or consultants as to the best thing to do. The choice of options may be influenced by religious, financial, social, medical, psychological, and probability factors—any of which can lead to difficult impasses. Sometimes the physician cannot successfully mediate in these discussions, and the courts may come into play. However, it has been my experience that almost always the physician *can* get an agreement between the parties if enough time is spent in careful and detailed discussion, and it is the doctor's responsibility to attempt this. If the conflict is between the patient and the family, the doctor can explain and support the patient's position. The patient should ask for this help when necessary.

What are my rights?

The physician has an obligation to discuss with you all the patient rights that were outlined in Chapter 2. Too often patients are not aware of their rights because they are insufficiently educated on the subject or they hesitate to raise such questions. The patient should ask the physician for open discussion about options and rights.

If I am suffering intolerably, will you talk with me about how death may be hastened?

Ask your doctor very specifically about what he or she is willing to do in the event you wish to hasten your death because of intolerable suffering. (This complicated topic is discussed in Chapters 7 through 9.) You should expect your doctor to be able to discuss these questions with you. If you are not satisfied with the answers you get, you always have the option to get another physician who is more empathetic to your wishes. Many patients hesitate to bring up such questions for fear of rejection or disapproval, but often patients are gratified by understanding responses from their doctor. You will never know if you do not ask.

WHAT YOU CAN EXPECT FROM THE NURSE IN END-OF-LIFE CARE

The nurse delivers an authoritative and comforting message to patients and families at the end of life. In recent decades, the nurse increasingly is the expert in assessing and managing medical treatment and partnering with the physician in these tasks. He or she often has frequent and prolonged contact with the patient, more so than the physician. This fosters the tendency of the patient to confide fears and ask questions of the nurse, who is in a position to set the tone for the end-of-life services offered to the patient.

Your physician and nurse should work together as a seamless team that allows the best use of each of their capabilities. I had the good fortune to work for a number of years in association with Ruth Porter, a nurse practitioner who had a large impact on the care of patients in our practice. She and I conferred multiple times daily about the needs of our patients and what should be done to meet those needs, and patients came to regard the two of us as a single entity to whom they could turn. Contacts with patients were often alternated between us, especially in chronically or terminally ill patients, and she seemed particularly expert and effective in dealing with the many kinds of discomfort that would plague patients. She was more easily able to spend the time necessary to investigate and follow up on the myriad details that make up effective comfort care and was an essential partner in caring for patients at the end of life. Between the two of us, we were able to provide this care regularly at home.

The nurse has this critical role to play, not only in private practices as Ruth Porter did with me, but also in visiting nurse associations, nursing homes, hospice organizations, the general hospital, and the intensive care unit. In all these settings, the nurse has a special ability to provide the patient with the sense of caring and compassion that is so needed at the end of life.

You can discuss with the nurse the type of nursing care available in these various settings for care that we discussed in Chapters 3 and 4 on comfort care, and at the same time inquire about the nurse's willingness to support a hastened death if this were ever deemed desirable.

The need is clear for well-integrated teams of physicians and nurses that serve as the preferred model for delivery of medical care across the whole spectrum of health care, certainly including end-of-life care. Whether the nurse has the extra qualifications and training of a nurse practitioner and perhaps is acting as your primary health care provider, is a specialist in some arena of nursing or hospice care, or is a generalist, he or she can be a source of great comfort to you and your family in dealing with end-of-life issues. All the questions we discussed earlier in the chapter that might be asked of the physician can with equal benefit be asked of the nurse. The modern nurse plays a vastly more important role in the delivery of health care than in previous decades, and you can take advantage of this greatly changed role.

A Final Thought about the System

As you discuss all the various questions and expectations with your caregivers, you may find that the medical system stands in the way. The delivery system for medical care in this country has been changing drastically in ways that are not necessarily conducive to the sort of personal interaction with doctors that we all want. We are often met with the pronouncement "that's just the way the system works" and told that we have to accommodate to reality. This is true to some extent, but I believe this response should always be resisted. Patients and families can and should stand up for their rights and expect a medical care system that is personalized and tailored to the needs of the individual. Insisting on this can go a long way toward making it a reality and will increase the likelihood of a relatively peaceful dying.

6

FAMILY AND FRIENDS

~⚬~⚬~

Often, in the physician's office, a patient who is in great need of help protests, "I could not ask my neighbor/friend/family to do that!" People in our society often seem reluctant to ask for needed help, yet doing so will often get the desired assistance and, additionally, will reward the person offering help. Friends and family like to be asked to help in difficult situations since it makes them feel as if they are doing something constructive. If excluded from helping, they can feel emotionally and psychologically out of the loop, and, when the patient has died, will have greater difficulty coping with the aftermath than if they had been allowed to participate in the process. This is a time to tell friends and family how they could be of assistance, and you should not feel "I'm just being a burden." Doing this is comforting for both of you, and not only will you feel less isolated, your friends and family will feel less helpless.

THE VALUE OF ALLOWING HELP TO BE GIVEN AT THE END

The terminal phase of life can be extremely important emotionally for patients, family, and friends. Sometimes the patient feels that the very last few weeks are best skipped and death should be hastened, but more frequently the very end can be incredibly important and poignant. My friend, Charles Baron, a professor of law at Boston College and an authority on the legal aspects of the end of life, told me of the death of his first wife.

"Her name was Irma. Yes, you can use her name and refer to her specifically. It would be a way of honoring her memory.

"She and I had known each other since fifth grade. We started dating at age fifteen. What a wonderful person! She grew up in the 1950s, graduated from college, and was one of that transition generation of women. When the kids got older, she started working part-time and then full-time, but always saw herself as a nurturer—principally wife and mother. Irma was just, competent, intelligent. She poured it all into taking care of us. Did a great job.

"Irma was sick for eight years. After the breast cancer diagnosis was made, she had a mastectomy and prophylactic chemotherapy. Four years later, the cancer came back, and she developed metastases to other areas. We knew unless some incredible breakthrough happened, she would soon be terminal, but Irma fought bravely at every turn and soldiered on through everything—and we tried it all.

"We did our last family trip to western Massachusetts, and it was very tough for her. She became bedridden. She had been fighting it all along, but now was an ill person, labeled as such in her mind. Irma felt as if she had gone from a healthy nurturer who was fighting cancer to a sick person who was dying and was dependent on others. She became very despondent, and we really had to work, the three kids and I, to convince her she was not a burden at all. It was the opposite. In a horrible way it was a gift in that we were honored to have this small opportunity to give back to her what she had done for us. For the remaining couple of months, it was an intimate time, a resumption of an intimacy we had not had in a long time, a way to communicate with one another, including the kids. The five of us were brought close together, and we felt wonderful about caring for her at home.

"In addition to hospice care, Irma was also under the care of friends and neighbors. A number of people were involved in caring for her when I was at the office. I think of one neighbor around the corner in particular. We hadn't been that close, and she came over to the house the first time to volunteer. I remember her frozen in the dining room, afraid to go upstairs to deal with Irma. We talked, and then she went upstairs and of course did beautifully—and kept coming back. Ever since, whenever we see each other, it's like an old buddy from a foxhole. We feel so close.

"There did come a point when Irma could have refused further treatment of a restorative sort and opted for giving in to an earlier death, but she didn't. Her blood count got very low, one lung collapsed, and she went to the hospital for a day or two, then came home again. Oxygen was used. This allowed those last couple of weeks to happen, and we were all glad. So, I am very careful when I talk to people about assisted suicide because we would have missed all of the above.

"Irma had become no longer embarrassed about our taking care of her physically and emotionally, but it took a lot of talking to get to that point. She learned to accept our care, and in doing so allowed us that period of intimacy. Although she didn't want the kids to remember her this way, we told her that we would remember her when she was beautiful. And we did."

What else is there left to say? This moving and poignant story illustrates to me how important it is for a dying patient to allow family and friends to participate meaningfully in end-of-life care. It contrasts with the choices of another friend who died with widely spread cancer.

She was in her fifties and was a good friend of my wife and mine, although we did not know her intimately. She had been health personified—a very active and vibrant person. However, she developed cancer that fairly rapidly became clearly incurable when it spread to various parts of her body. As she came closer and closer to her death—an obvious process—we inquired how she felt and how things were going. Her response was invariably "fine!" followed by an immediate change of subject. She was not comfortable with sharing any details of her illness with us, and she died without our being able to acknowledge to her our sorrow at her dying and the problems she was going through—but that was the way she wanted it.

Another friend in somewhat similar circumstances allowed us an entry into her problems, but on her terms—which was all right.

This friend had a chronic illness, which she managed with a stiff upper lip approach, successfully so. Early in the course of her illness, when I complained to her that she never let down her guard about her obvious illness, she agreed to talk about things in detail, but only on occasion—which we defined, literally, as once every six months. At those times, she would speak frankly about how she felt, and it was helpful to her and to us. In this way and in others she allowed us to help her as friends. It was a negotiated, but fine, compromise.

As this shows, people differ in how they wish to die just as they differ in their ways of living. While family and friends may wish to help and will feel more comfortable after the death if they have been a part of the process, it has to be on the patient's terms.

Letting the Patient Decide the Ground Rules

When we attempt to help a patient who is dying, we need to remember that this help and support should be given on rules (expressed or implicit) set by the patient. It is the patient who is dying, and it is the patient who needs the most comfort, so the patient should decide whom they wish to see, when, and for how long. Some will want visits from many family members. Some will want a no-holds barred discussion of everything: past, present, and future; personal emotional matters; factual matters of what to do with the bank account; and an exploration of difficult relationships in the past. Others will want a much more limited exploration of the disease, prognosis, emotions, and personal matters. The patient mentioned previously, who was always "fine," was in the latter category.

I am convinced, however, that if a friend or family member approaches the patient with antennae fully extended, it is possible to sense how much company the patient wants, what the patient wants to talk about, and what the patient wants to avoid. That should be the guiding rule. Respect the psychological background from which the patient comes, and pay attention to previously held religious and moral precepts. Make some gentle, physical contact, hold the patient's hand, sit close with your head on a level with the patient's, and speak of the good things he or she has meant to you, and you will do fine and will be a comfort.

Special Role of Family or Friend Who Is Also Designated Proxy Agent

The person appointed as the medical agent or proxy who will legally speak for you in matters of medical decision making when you are no longer able to do so on your own behalf (see Chapter 12) may be anyone: a professional (such as a family lawyer), a close friend, or a family member. There is a real advantage, however, when the agent is either a family member or a friend since this person tends to know you well and be more easily able to say what you would have wanted had you been able to participate in medical decision making. As we shall see later in this book, the appointment of a medical proxy can be accompanied by specific written instructions or not. If you sign the delegation of authority and leave the details up to the agent, rather than being highly specific with written details, you are assuming that the agent will know what you would have wanted—either by virtue of having discussed it while you were still competent or simply on the basis of knowing you well through the years. This is most likely to be the case when the agent has been either a family member or a close friend. When possible, it is wise for you to pick such a person when selecting a proxy because there is usually a stronger sense of trust that proper decisions will be made.

Emotional, Social, and Spiritual Needs

A whole book could be written on this subject, but here I shall simply say it is paramount that the patient's emotional and psychological needs be shepherded through the dying process as carefully as the physical needs. Family and friends should be encouraged to talk with the patient about dying and what it means to all concerned—while respecting the patient's wishes and sensitivities as we discussed previously. Once death is imminent, both patient and family are more likely to say things they have hesitated to bring up. A deep, heartfelt discussion can help all those involved experience a sense of completion and feel more peaceful and accepting.

Reminiscences about good times can be interspersed with the more difficult subject of the dying process itself and its various implications. The bottom line is that simply *talking substantively* with the patient is a critical part of comfort care.

When Family and Friends Disagree with the Patient

The decision to take the turning point toward comfort care is a decision that belongs to the patient, as long as he or she is able to participate in medical decision-making. Usually friends and family support the patient's desires, but this is not always the case. There may be significant disagreement. In this instance, complex psychological factors are at play, and the physician or other counselor may need to facilitate an understanding between the parties involved. Nevertheless, the definite bottom line with an end-of-life patient who is competent is that the patient's wishes are paramount. This legal right to make decisions about one's own health care directly or through an appointed proxy must trump any doubts and disagreements among those family and friends who surround the patient.

In my own experience as a physician, I have found that there is no need for these disagreements to lead to confrontation. Consensus building is much preferable and can usually be accomplished by means of open, respectful discussion led by the physician. I haven't seen a disagreement at the end of life that could not be resolved by a discussion among patient, family, and friends, although it does occur occasionally—and in such unfortunate circumstances, the courts often become involved.

7

The Second Turning Point: Making the Decision to Hasten Death

~ ✦ ~

At the end of life, if you are suffering intolerably even though all comfort measures have been applied, you and your family may feel that dying is preferable to living. If this is the case, you have reached the second turning point: the wish to hasten death. Making this decision can be very difficult, but there are ways to address it systematically.

A Terrible Outlook in a Patient with Cancer of the Tongue: What to Do for David?

Quite a few years ago, David developed cancer of the back of the tongue. He was a man in his early sixties who had long been a patient of mine. Although the growth had been treated, it had now returned, and the situation was serious. He was an outgoing person who always seemed to enjoy life, but as he sat in my office with his wife, Abigail, we all were dispirited.

The new and latest recurrence was interfering with his swallowing, and obstruction of his breathing passages was not far off. Further surgery had been considered but was not thought possible. He had had the maximum amount of radiation the area could tolerate, and at that time, chemotherapy for this particular growth was not an effective option. Because we had no definitive treatment that would cure or slow the cancer, comfort measures were all we had to offer, and his death would not be free of suffering.

I had not spoken to David and his wife about my fears, but inwardly I was extremely apprehensive about what he faced. It seemed to me that a very bad death—losing his ability to swallow, choking on his secretions, and having his airway compromised—lay ahead. Principally, I feared that his ability to breathe was going to be severely limited by the increasing size of the cancer mass, which would slowly cut off the air passage to his trachea and would interfere with his ability to handle normal respiratory secretions. This would cause him severe anxiety and agitation. It was not a matter of pain—we could treat pain with the management techniques that were then available. The problem was the distress David would experience as the growing cancer obstructed his airway passages and throat.

David was going to be one of those very occasional patients in a physician's lifetime practice who, in spite of the best possible care, still suffers unrelieved and intolerable distress, such that the patient prefers death over continued living. The unrelenting misery cannot be sufficiently dealt with by even the best of comfort measures. This situation goes beyond physical pain, which may or may not be present. I was convinced that this was going to be the case with David. He had not at that point said anything about hastening his death, but he was clearly apprehensive about the future.

We sat there for some moments without saying anything. David broke the troubled silence by broaching the subject so far unaddressed. He said, "This whole thing is so discouraging. I want to end my life soon and not go through all that's ahead. I've been afraid to bring it up."

He had researched his options and told his wife and me that he could end his own life by taking a large dose of Seconal (a barbiturate that then was used primarily as a sleeping medication for insomnia). There was another silence, as he looked first at me and then his wife. I knew what he was talking about and knew privately that, if I were in his shoes, I would be thinking the same way. He then informed us that he had accumulated a sufficient dose of the medication. If he took all the capsules he had, within minutes he would be asleep, and within a very few hours his breathing would stop.

David's statement jarred Abigail. She wanted to support him in any way, but she had never addressed, in her own mind, the thought of his ending his life. I felt unable to advise him on this subject (this was early in my career, and I was still trying to formulate my own position on such a matter), but I told him I would try to relieve his distress as the next few weeks went by, principally by using large doses of morphine to dull his symptoms and awareness. I said that if very large doses of morphine were needed, this might, as a consequence of treating his severe symptoms, shorten his life by some hours or days but that I would use whatever was required to keep him comfortable. I told him that if he decided he wanted to use the Seconal on his own to end his suffering sooner, it had to be his decision and his action.

David's consultants and other caregivers to that point had done everything right. Throughout the previous several years, he had been seen by multiple specialists at one of the very best cancer facilities in Boston. He was twice brought back to reasonable health by aggressive intervention, but now, when cure seemed no longer possible, he had recognized and dealt with the questions of the first turning point and elected comfort care only. He, Abigail, his cancer specialists, and I redefined the goal of his treatment: We would shepherd him through his dying process with as much peacefulness as possible. All of his caregivers continued to provide meticulous and frequent attention, and as his family physician, I certainly did not pull back from the situation just because we were stopping efforts to cure. David's psychological needs increased, and they were met in the best way possible by everyone around him. His moderate pain was controlled with strong medication in big enough and frequent enough doses. David had no unwanted tube feedings or intravenous fluids (we had a clear understanding that we were not to use these), and all medications were stopped, except those needed for comfort.

We had addressed all of the big and little problems of comfort care in the best way possible, yet this seriously bad future still loomed ahead.

I was thankful that David had the knowledge and wherewithal to develop the Seconal option on his own, to be used if things went as poorly as I expected. Still educating myself about end-of-life options at that time, I was not sure what I would do had he not raised the issue himself.

Over the next couple of weeks, David, Abigail, and I met several more times, and each time David reiterated his wish to hasten his death. David was absolutely clear in his mind that a planned death was what he wanted, and his tenacity in this belief reassured Abigail to the point that she supported him in this wish. Abigail had only one proviso: "I do not want to know, David, when you are going to take medication to do this. I love you, and want for you what you want, but *you* have to do this." David understood, and gently and courageously told her that he did. I listened to all of this, but did not counsel them about the decision. They came to it on their own.

A few days after that, Abigail telephoned me at 6 AM to say she thought David had died. I immediately went to their house and found him looking perfectly peaceful—fully dressed, lying on his side with his hands folded together under one cheek—as if he had simply gone to sleep. He had died quietly by his own hand. I was relieved and so was Abigail. David's trials were over at a time and in a manner of his own choosing. The only thing I regret about his death now, years later, is that he died alone. Even though Abigail had not wanted to know or be present, many doctors now would encourage her to allow a trusted person to be with her husband when he ended his life.

David was like many at the end of life. After the first turning point had been reached and agreed upon, he had been too afraid to ask his doctor about all the possible options for shortening the period of suffering. Today, your physician may be more aware than I was those years ago. These questions need to be raised in a proactive way.[1] However, some physicians still will not raise the subject with those patients who have not been able to broach the issue on their own. Even if the patient is the one to raise the question of hastening death by an overdose of barbiturate, the use of helium (discussed more fully in Chapter 9), or other overt and clear-cut means, the doctor may still evade the question or state frankly that he cannot help. However, with the passage of time, further education, and a more permissive legal environment, this is changing so that the option of hastened death is more often easily discussed in these dire situations.

Properly given comfort care ensures that the overwhelming majority of patients do not wish to hasten death. This is vital to emphasize. Patients are not likely to consider the options for a planned, earlier death until optimal comfort care has been given but is no longer effective. Although vigorously applied pain and comfort measures should suffice to provide a peaceful death in the vast majority of instances, patients and families need to be prepared to deal with the infrequent situation when intolerable distress persists in spite of all usual measures, as was about to happen in David's case. In these instances, the situation declares itself and is undeniable. Hastening death means ultimate control for some people facing the end of life: the right to determine when and under what circumstances they can end intolerable suffering after all other options have been exhausted.

Hastening death is part of a spectrum of end-of-life care. It is not suicide in the usual sense, in that the principal cause of death is the basic disease process that has brought a patient to the brink of death. Planning a death on one's own terms does not take away from the causality of the underlying disease.

How Have Decisions for Hastened Death Been Made? Questions That Must Be Asked

In the following two chapters we shall go over each of the options that have been used for hastening death, but before doing so, we should consider the questions that patients and families have asked in order to decide whether this could be the best course and a proper action.

In the past, others and I have outlined suggested safeguards for any action that might hasten death.[2] A series of questions have been asked by patients to be sure rational decisions were made. If the answers to the following questions were all "yes," then patients and families facing this dilemma probably have been reasonably comfortable and at peace with a planned death. These essential and mandatory questions have been raised appropriately not only by those who wished to discontinue unwanted treatment (in favor of comfort care only) but also by those who sought more aggressive measures for hastening death.

(Note that in the Oregon law permitting physicians in that state to give assistance in dying, many of these questions are codified in the law as formal requirements. The law is discussed in detail in Appendix B. This groundbreaking referendum makes it legal for physicians to aid patients who wish to hasten death under certain circumstances, and numerous safeguards are built in to prevent any abuse. The law applies only in Oregon, although several other states are looking at enacting similar legislation.)

Here are the issues patients in the past have properly addressed with their caregivers when they wished for a hastened death. The first eight relate to whether all other options that would relieve suffering have been considered carefully and judged not to be helpful or possible.

1. Have all acceptable options for treatment of the basic disease been exhausted? In the case of malignant disease, have further surgery, radiation, chemotherapy, hormone treatments, and other possible basic treatments that aim to cure or at least improve the patient's condition been considered? (This does not mean that every possible treatment should be offered or undertaken, but rather those treatments that have a reasonable chance for success. In an earlier chapter of this book, we address the question of how one decides what is reasonable, a decision that depends largely on the degree of probabilities with which one is comfortable. This is an individual choice on which people will differ.)

2. If pain is present, has it been addressed with modern techniques of pain control? Very few instances occur in which pain cannot be controlled satisfactorily if remedial measures are aggressive and modern in approach. Specialists in pain control can assist the regular doctor in this effort, and their services should be employed when ordinary pain control measures do not suffice. Rarely should a patient wish for hastened death because of pain that cannot be controlled—although very occasionally this does happen.

3. Apart from pain per se, one may suffer a high degree of misery and distress that makes one wish for life to be at an end. Have all the aspects of such distress been analyzed to see what can be relieved, and how? Has aggressive action been taken to relieve all the factors that are susceptible to relief?

4. Have all consultants been called in who might offer some form of relief for the conditions causing the intolerable distress? Have second opinions been pursued in cases of doubt about some issue?

5. Has clinical depression been ruled out? This question is discussed in Chapter 10. Most people experience appropriate

sadness near the end of life, and this is different from clinical depression, which is usually amenable to various treatment measures. If depression seems to be a problem, proper consultation and treatment should be sought since depression may and usually does aggravate feelings of intolerable suffering.

6. Have all the services offered by hospice, home care programs, social service consultants, and other service organizations been utilized to their maximum? Patients with desperately bad situations that produce a sense of hopelessness can often better tolerate their plight if they have sufficient psychological and physical help.

7. Has comfort care been applied with intensity and great attention to detail in all areas?

8. Is the suffering person fully informed about all alternatives?

9. Has a second physician confirmed that the disease process is in a terminal stage? In end-of-life issues, *terminal* refers to a disease process that will lead to death in six months. Many people have argued that the right to hasten death should not be restricted solely to patients with terminal disease. They feel that patients who have an intolerable, irremediable disease or condition, such as quadriplegia or the threat of future dementia, which is not terminal, should be granted the same autonomy over the manner and place of dying as is possessed by a terminal patient. This proposition will take time to resolve, and at present most ethicists and legislators do not defend it. Therefore, I am staying with terminal disease as being a proper criterion for hastened death, although hopefully in the near future, a broader and more liberal position will evolve—a change I would support.

10. Is the patient competent to decide? For Alzheimer's disease and other forms of dementia, we need better answers that will probably require legislative action, but this will take time. I presently have no good answer for hastened death in dementia since the voluntary hastening of death requires

the patient to have the mental capacity to make an informed decision and to carry out the act himself or herself, and that—by definition—is usually impossible with Alzheimer's. It is difficult for such a patient to determine a time for hastening death since, by the time things are obvious, the patient is often beyond the point of being able to carry out the desired measures. In 2005, I participated in an attempt to work out some guidelines for this particularly difficult problem with a group of physicians, attorneys, and lay persons in the Boston area.[3] An essential question to address is the matter of "precommitment."[4] How can (with respect to hastening death) a present competent self have the authority to bind with an advance directive aimed at a future noncompetent self? What if the incompetent self wants to continue to live? With which self should family and doctors side? There is no easy answer. In Chapter 11, we discuss further the use of a special advance directive for Alzheimer's disease and other forms of dementia that, if enabled by new legislation, could help resolve this dilemma.

11. Is a person contemplating hastened dying fully informed and understanding about what is involved in a hastened death? Is the decision clearly and completely voluntary?

12. Does the degree of suffering warrant ending life prematurely? Is the suffering intolerable? The definition of the amount of suffering that is intolerable is a subjective one for which people will have different answers. What is intolerable for one person may not be for another. This is as it should be, and the definition of intolerable suffering should be left to the individual. It does not have to involve intolerable pain since other problems can cause suffering: fear of pain, fear of losing control, loss of dignity, generalized discomfort and distress, profound weakness, persistent and severe nausea, and other symptoms that may take away any sense of quality of life. What is important is the amount of suffering *perceived* by the patient.

13. Does the suffering patient believe there will be minimal deleterious effects on the survivors from a decision to end life in a planned, hastened way? The answer to this question in most instances depends on the degree to which family and friends have been prepared for the act of hastening death. When a hastened death occurs, there is the possibility that survivors will have feelings of anger, guilt, or regret—all of which at times may be severe. However, if survivors understand ahead of time the reasons for the hastened death, these feelings should be minimal or nonexistent. The primary feeling usually is one of relief that the suffering for their loved one is over. When discussion about the act ahead of time is possible, this is most often all that is necessary to enable survivors to feel comfortable. Sometimes, however, people choose to proceed in secrecy when they know or suspect family members are opposed, but it is better to try to "talk it out" ahead of time so that survivors can be understanding and supportive.

14. Has every effort been made to have the physician closely involved in any move toward a planned, hastened death? Although some doctors will not be supportive because they believe for legal, ethical, or religious reasons they cannot advise about options for hastening death, patients are often surprised by the empathetic response from their doctor when the subject is broached. Involvement of the personal physician is tremendously reassuring to the patient, but unfortunately legal constraints are a big consideration when the physician thinks of having any role in a death that goes beyond simply withdrawing treatment, using large doses of morphine to treat severe symptoms of distress or pain, or treating symptoms in a patient who has elected to forgo fluids (a means of hastening death that we discuss later in this book). The physician in many jurisdictions can arguably be potentially liable legally if he or she actually assists in a suicide or discusses options for suicide with the patient in a

manner that appears more advisory than merely informative. The line here may be a thin one, and the physician needs to exercise caution to avoid crossing it. The cautious physician, wishing to remain on the safe side of the law, will probably provide factual, historical information rather than deliver instructions or advice prospectively as to what should be done.

Many physicians may *perceive* legal risk (even in situations clearly within the law) and thereby are reluctant to discuss the matter. If sufficient information cannot be obtained, you have every right to change medical care to a doctor who will support your wishes in whatever legal ways he or she can. Hopefully, however, you have already ascertained earlier in your relationship with your doctor his or her general feelings on this matter.

15. Lastly, patients have had to decide whether they feel morally and ethically at ease with hastening death. No one should press their own values on a patient. There are people who, for religious or ethical considerations, feel they could never purposely end their own life. Many believe that no one other than God has the right or power to decide when life begins or ends. A decision to hasten death would be very difficult for such a person. Each person should have the right to make a decision that is consistent with his or her own beliefs, and no religious organization should have the last word.

Those who have had some indecision on this last point have benefited from remarks made by Bishop John Shelby Spong, Episcopal Bishop in the diocese of Newark, in a keynote address to the Hemlock USA (predecessor to End-of-Life Choices, now Compassion and Choices) meeting in San Diego on January 10, 2003. He said, in part:

"I believe that if and when a person arrives at that point in human existence when death has become a kinder alternative than hopeless pain and when a chronic dependency on narcotics begins to require the loss of personal dignity, then the basic human right to choose how and when to die should be guaranteed by law and respected by our communities of faith. . . .

"In the course of our history, we Christians have never left the power to die exclusively in God's hands. Rather we have fought religious wars in which people were killed quite deliberately . . . The records of history show that Christian rulers in ostensibly Christian nations, aided and abetted by the prevailing religious hierarchies of the Christian churches, have shown no reluctance whatsoever in claiming the right to take the power of life and death from God's hands and to place that power squarely into their own very human hands. . . .

"When medical science shifts from expanding the length and quality of life and begins simply to postpone the reality of death, why are we not capable of saying that the sacredness of life is no longer being served, and therefore Christians must learn to act responsibly in the final moments of life? . . . Do we human beings, including those of us who claim to be Christians, not have the right to say 'that is not the way I choose to die'? I believe we do! . . .

"I think this choice should be legal. I will work, therefore, through the political processes to seek to create a world where advance directives are obeyed and where physicians will assist those who choose to do so, with the ability to die at the appropriate time. I also think the choice to do this should be acclaimed as both moral and ethical, a human right if you will. . . ."

You may take comfort from these arguments of Bishop Spong if hastening death is being considered. There is no reason for religion to stand in the way of the autonomy that is deserved. Being religious and believing in autonomy at the end of life are not inconsistent positions.

In the past, when these questions discussed in the last few pages have all been addressed individually and each has been resolved with a "yes" answer or at least has been properly considered, patients who faced intolerable and unrelieved suffering were able more easily to make a decision as to whether they should undertake a course of action aimed at hastening death.

SUMMARY OF ARGUMENTS FOR PLANNED, HASTENED DEATH IN THE INTOLERABLY SUFFERING PATIENT

The death with dignity movement has regularly come under attack from some who use questionable logic in their opposition to physician aid-in-dying. The following points can be considered in countering their criticisms.

1. The right to choose the time and manner of your dying is a matter of personal autonomy. Case law (the body of court decisions that sets precedent) in this country usually supports concepts of autonomy of the individual.

2. At the end of life, if you choose to hasten death in a terminal disease, you are freely exercising a choice and preference. Nothing is forced. People who choose not to hasten their deaths are under no pressure whatever to do so. The Oregon law very explicitly guards against this, effectively so, and there has been no abuse in this regard. In the same way that proponents of the option of hastened death do not impose their beliefs on others, those who do not wish this option should not deny the right to others who do.

3. Hastening death should be an option only when suffering is intolerable and cannot be relieved by usual treatment. It is considered only when all else has failed. The need for hastened death is an extremely occasional one because comfort care is now so advanced and improved. There does, however, remain the very infrequent situation in which the suffering patient justifiably can request assistance in ending life.

4. The Oregon experience (we address this in detail later in Appendix B) indicates that there is no rush of patients to avail themselves of this option. The number of people who have used the law remains very small in comparison to the

overall death rate. No abuses have been observed by state authorities in Oregon, and there is no evidence that legalization of physician aid in dying creates a "slippery slope" of abuse of this option.

5. The experience in Oregon has shown that legalization of physician aid-in-dying leads to improved overall care of the dying, such that now Oregon leads all other states in several important measurements of the quality of comfort care.[5]

6. Assisting a person in ending life *should* be considered part of the spectrum of treatment for the dying patient. For those whose intolerable suffering cannot be relieved, ending life can be the most humane and compassionate treatment.

7. There is no inconsistency between being a devoutly religious person and favoring legalized aid-in-dying.

8

What Options Have Been Used in the Past to Hasten Death?

❧❧

Now that we have seen how an intolerably suffering patient might make a decision to hasten death, we need to examine the methods by which this has been done in the past. There are some methods that have produced real problems and others that have led to relatively peaceful and certain deaths.

Any person who has intolerable suffering and who wishes the end of life to be hastened has already recognized the first turning point and has substituted comfort care for attempts to cure.

What can be done beyond that if suffering persists intolerably at the second turning point, when a person feels that death is preferable to continued living?

Methods Used in the Past That Are Often Unsuccessful or Problematic

1. *The use of a gun or other violent method* to commit suicide is at times a choice patients think of when they do not know what else to do. Too often the attempt does not succeed, and aftereffects on surviving family and friends make this painful emotionally.
2. *The use of carbon monoxide* from automobile exhaust in a closed garage has been used for many years as a method for

ending life, but it frequently fails. While it is true that carbon monoxide in a high enough concentration is lethal, there are too many occasions in which people attempt this method to end suffering only to find that a variety of mechanical and logistical problems frustrates their attempt, and the attempt simply makes them sick or produces brain damage without ending life.

3. *Stopping eating (starvation)* has been very slow and protracted as a means of ending life. Although persons with terminal illness who have tried this method have lost weight due to reduced food intake, the avoiding of food in order to end life has been drawn out and difficult emotionally for both patient and family. However, discontinuing of all *fluids*, thereby inducing terminal dehydration, has been a successful option, as we shall see later in this book.

4. *Euthanasia* is so clearly illegal in the United States that it is not considered here as an option in this country—although some physicians or nurses witnessing great suffering do it secretly, and distraught family members have also resorted to euthanasia by one method or another. Euthanasia is an overt, physical act, such as that of a physician who administers a lethal injection of some sort, that ends the life of the patient at that very time. Euthanasia is different from physician aid-in-dying, as practiced legally in Oregon, in that the physician in the latter instance does not actually perform a physical act that causes death at the time; instead, the patient must himself or herself perform the actual physical act (e.g., ingestion of a lethal dose of medication or performing the physical acts necessary to end life with helium [see Chapter 9 on helium]). I believe that euthanasia, as performed in The Netherlands (see Appendix C), should become a legal possibility for patients in the United States, but that is not going to happen anytime in the near future.

SUCCESSFUL MEANS BY WHICH SUFFERING HAS BEEN SHORTENED AND DEATH HASTENED

1. *Withdrawal of unwanted treatment and procedures.* The stopping of any intrusive or unwanted therapy has been part of the basic change of approach at the first turning point—a result of the decision to render comfort care only. Unwanted measures can include artificial nutrition or a respirator. Discontinuing treatment has been discussed in the chapter on comfort care, and has been a self-evident first step. There is no legal or ethical problem when a competent patient or a duly appointed agent of an incompetent patient refuses unwanted treatment.

2. *Administration of morphine and sedating medications in whatever large doses are necessary to relieve the intolerable suffering.* At times, this has meant that life is shortened by the medications needed to produce relief.

3. *Voluntary refusal of all hydration (fluids) leading to terminal dehydration and an earlier death.* To be successful, this needs to be accompanied by a doctor's administering any needed medication for distress or pain.

4. *Aid-in-dying from the physician in the form of prescribing barbiturates to be taken by the patient (physician aid-in-dying).* This is the approach that has been used legally in Oregon.

5. *The use of helium.* This is a new mechanical means of hastening death that has not necessarily required physician involvement.

The first three options listed above are generally regarded as legal in any jurisdiction, but the last two have legal issues, as we shall see. In this chapter, we shall describe these options in more detail except for withdrawal of unwanted treatment, which has been covered earlier in this book, and the discussion of helium, which is covered in the next chapter.

Increasing Doses of Morphine

In the chapter on comfort care, we addressed Marie's situation in which she discontinued unwanted treatment after the first turning point was defined. (You may recall that she had rejected continued tube feedings when her cancer of the esophagus was no longer able to be checked in any way.) Her case pointed out the important role of increasing doses of morphine used to control general restlessness, anxiety, and any possible sensations of thirst—in addition to controlling her pain. In Marie's case, the large morphine doses necessary were associated (probably) with an earlier death, but they allowed her last few days to pass in relative peace since the morphine put her into a somnolent state in which she was largely unaware of her distressing situation.

Morphine is an old but still frequently used medication. Many physicians feel that if they could have only one drug to treat end-of-life distress, it would be morphine; generations of doctors have successfully given it in increasing doses when the usually prescribed doses do not suffice to relieve pain or distress in terminal illness. In this setting, the dose of morphine has been ethically and legally pushed to the point necessary to relieve distress, even if life is shortened by hours or days due to the respiratory depression that morphine may cause. Many dying patients have had their dying eased in this manner. Using morphine in this setting is an appropriate and compassionate move by the physician and remains one of the important legal options for such patients.

Physicians have recognized that in patients who have chronic pain and who are already receiving large, steady doses of morphine, the amount of increased morphine necessary to relieve suffering may be great. With prolonged use, patients develop a tolerance not only to the pain-relieving characteristic of morphine, but also to the side effects of morphine, such as depression of respiration.

The Double Effect Rationale When Increasing Doses of Morphine Hastens Death

When morphine is used in large doses with the intent of relieving severe symptoms in the terminal patient, and when death is hastened by some hours or days by these large doses, physicians have in the past relied on the "double effect" rationale to justify the action. As you discuss end-of-life options with your doctors and nurses, you may hear this term, which is why I have included it here. The double-effect rationale holds that it is ethical to use doses of a medication that will most likely shorten life if the intent is solely to treat severe symptoms. Some physicians and ethicists, however, have argued that it is probably hypocritical not to acknowledge what is being done and not to call it physician aid-in-dying.

Charles Baron, a professor of law at Boston College and an expert on end-of-life problems, opposes the use of the double-effect rationale as the basis for allowing hastened death under the guise of relieving symptoms.[1] He feels that if we are really opposed to euthanasia, we would not permit physicians to hasten death "incidentally" with large doses of pain medication, and he does not believe this rationale is good for our legal system, society, the medical profession, or patients. He does not oppose the use of morphine in large doses to relieve suffering, but wants us to be clear in our thinking about what can happen with large doses and not hide behind double-effect justification—which he regards as convoluted.[2]

Garrick F. Cole, a Boston attorney who is also an expert in end-of-life issues, feels that it is a distortion to use the concept of double effect.[3] He feels it is unnecessary to go beyond our already accepted use of potentially dangerous medications with side effects when the goal is to relieve symptoms, and the use is an informed one. Cole points out that if the patient wishes to, and needs to, run the risk of side effects of a given medication, such as morphine in large doses, and if the medication is needed for the welfare of the patient, the physician can go ahead with the administration of the medication. He contends that we do this all the time on the basis that the side effects of treatment are ethically and legally acceptable if the risks are known and accepted. Cole regards the double-effect doctrine as unnecessary and argues that if the physician is using very large doses of morphine to control severe symptoms at the end of life and if the physician and patient would at the same time be gratified by a hastened death, there should be no legal or ethical problem with admitting these goals openly. He sees this as a more honest approach as opposed to utilizing the doctrine of double effect and not admitting that an earlier death would be welcomed.

However, for a physician to admit openly to using morphine at the patient's request in such a dose that death will probably be hastened puts that physician, at least in the minds of some, in perceived legal jeopardy, and few physicians want to do this. So, although doubts about the validity of the double-effect justification have been expressed by some, most physicians in practice, including myself, are comfortable with it. This dilemma of double-effect justification for shortening life would be solved by allowing the physician and patient to shorten life openly when suffering is intolerable and unrelieved—with legal protection and guidelines of Oregon-like laws in all jurisdictions (discussed in Appendix B). Hopefully, this will come about in the next decade.

In the meantime, we should be careful not to get too hung up about intent if this results in less good care for the suffering patient. Rod McStay at Methodist Hospital in Houston points out in an extensive and scholarly monograph that "the current alternative to using the double effect principle as a legal justification . . . is the under-treatment of pain for patients that are unresponsive to typical levels of medication. It would be an unfortunate consequence if scrutiny . . . about clinical intentions resulted in inadequate palliative care for patients."[4] In the article, McStay was speaking primarily about terminal sedation (see the following section), but the same reasoning applies to the use of high doses of morphine for intolerable symptoms.

Along the same line, Timothy Quill states, when discussing the double effect in his book *A Midwife Through the Dying Process: Stories of Healing and Hard Choices at the End of Life,* "Our primary intention was to relieve his suffering, not to cause his death, so we were still operating under the confines of the 'double effect.' Yet, in reality, relieving his suffering and easing death had become one."[5] One should not have to choose between the two.

A physician runs a very low likelihood of being criminally charged with murder when using the double effect rationale, but the risk is not zero. Ann Alpers, JD, assistant professor of medicine in the Program in Medical Ethics and the Division of Internal Medicine in the Department of Medicine, University of California, San Francisco, wrote a detailed scholarly paper on the risks incurred by physicians as they attempt to relieve suffering at the end of life with heavy doses of medications, especially those that are "closely regulated by state and federal law."[6]

Pointing out that a crime usually has two basic elements: A criminal act has been performed, and it has been intentional, Alpers searched the legal literature for all instances of "criminal investigations and actions brought against physicians for care, particularly pain control, at the end of life." She eliminated situations in which the physician "showed gross or culpable departures from the ordinary standard of care," focusing rather on the narrowed subject of pain control at the end of life in which the double effect doctrine might be relevant. She found that "even though criminal prosecutions of physicians [for giving such heavy doses of medication that life was shortened] are still rare, they have become more common in the United States within the past ten years."

Alpers found (since 1990) "a total of at least twenty-three investigations of professional caregivers, eight indictments, four murder trials, and two physician convictions. One set of convictions (for attempted first-degree murder and second-degree murder) was reversed on appeal."[7] (See the extensive note at the end of the book for a discussion of this interesting case.) All the cases involved an informant who reported concerns about how the patient died. Alpers noted that these "prosecutions arising from care of the dying and attempts to manage pain in the terminally ill fall into three broad categories: withdrawal of life-sustaining treatment and any accompanying use of pain medication; the administration of morphine or other analgesics and sedatives; and terminal care that includes the use of a potentially fatal agent, such as potassium chloride, insulin, or chloroform."

As I looked at these cases, some common threads seemed to stand out. I thought physicians were less likely to get into serious legal difficulty if they met the following desirable criteria:

1. The patient was competent to make the medical decision voluntarily to withdraw unwanted treatment at the end of life and to have medication in whatever doses necessary for relief of pain and/or distress.

2. The patient asked for these actions in a written advance directive, such that, if the actions took place later at a time when the patient was no longer able to speak for himself or herself, a properly designated medical agent was able to make such decisions, acting in the patient's best interest.

3. The use of morphine or other distress-relieving drugs—in whatever dose was necessary to control the symptom(s)—occurred in situations in which these drugs were clinically necessary to relieve pain, distress, or agitation that was otherwise uncontrollable.

4. The physician was extremely clear in the written medical records as to exactly what he/she was doing and why, detailing how the actions were requested by the patient voluntarily (either directly or through an appointed agent), how they were in the best interests of the patient, how there

were no other reasonable options, and how the actions represented the only compassionate course.

5. Families were totally informed and understanding of, and agreeable to, what the physician was doing and why.

When these criteria were met, it appeared that the risk for criminal prosecution was very small and truly negligible for any physician who withdrew treatment and administered symptom-relieving medication in large doses to a dying patient with unrelieved suffering.

Further, it appeared to me that the physicians who avoided running into trouble with prosecutors and court actions used very standard pain-relieving or sedating medications, and did not utilize medications that paralyze muscle action or directly stop the heartbeat. These medications in my opinion are not required for the relief of pain and/or distress at the end of life.

The unfortunate thing is that even when the physician acts in a way that is highly unlikely to bring any legal action, he or she may still worry about risk and as a consequence undertreat end-of-life pain and distress. The specter of legal sanction hangs over the head of any physician who uses large doses of pain-relieving medication, even when the statistical likelihood of sanction is remote.

VOLUNTARY REFUSAL OF HYDRATION, ACCOMPANIED BY PHYSICIAN-ADMINISTERED SEDATION AS NEEDED

Voluntary refusal of hydration is a possible next step. Refusing fluids leads to dehydration, which, in turn, produces somnolence. The somnolence can be further aided by physician-administered sedation, as needed. If necessary, the patient is put to sleep and kept in this peaceful state until death, which usually occurs in a matter of days. All of this is completely legal when done for the relief of intolerable suffering.

Patients have a right to refuse fluids just as they have a right to refuse unwanted medical treatment. To give fluids against a competent patient's wish could be considered battery. Physician and family should support such a decision by the patient and point out to all caregivers that this is a legal right.

Deliberately refusing hydration is a decision patients have used successfully in the past, and it is a procedure that is having increased use. (Note that this refusal of hydration is more effective than starvation, which is not a good way to hasten death because it is slow and difficult.) Particularly in patients who already have considerable biochemical abnormalities due to terminal illness, the stopping of all fluids can clearly bring on an earlier death, sometimes in a matter of only a few days and almost never longer than ten (depending on the person's condition).

Many people die with dehydration as part of the normal disease process of a fatal illness that prevents taking food or drink.[8] Dehydration in such cases is expected and can be accepted as part of a natural way of dying. There is no medical mandate to provide hydration in terminal patients, since hydration may simply prolong dying.

There are misperceptions about dehydration and its symptomatic effect on the dying patient. If a normal, healthy person forgoes fluids, extreme thirst and distress is indeed soon experienced. This is not true in the dying patient, who experiences dehydration quite differently. When a patient is close to dying, the illness and the dying process impose a form of auto-sedation in which all the senses are dulled, including the sensation of thirst. Insufficient understanding of this phenomenon leads dying patients and their families to discount unnecessarily this avenue as a possible option at the end of life.

Dehydration per se does not have to be a distressing state. Lethargy and somnolence are symptoms of dehydration, and somnolence may be helpful in that it reduces awareness of distress. Dehydration may bring about increased production of endorphins, chemicals in the body that are helpful in that they may be an important cause of this reduced awareness. As for dryness of the mouth, meticulous mouth care can counter this problem, and other symptoms arising from the underlying fatal disease process can be treated effectively with sufficient doses of medication.

Nevertheless, the medical literature has contained many discussions in the last twenty years concerning the question of the patient's reaction to dehydration—is it detrimental or beneficial to the patient's comfort? The arguments on both sides were well reviewed in 2001 by Diana McAulay, a staff nurse in England.[9] I believe the pendulum has swung clearly in the direction of believing the somnolence and lethargy associated with dehydration to be beneficial to the dying patient—actually easing the dying process. More hospice workers and palliative care experts are coming around to this opinion,[10] and this shift in opinion definitely fits with my own experience. I have personally attended many dying patients during four decades of practice of internal medicine, and I have never seen the bad consequences of dehydration painted by those who speak against this option for the dying patient—as long as proper oral care and other indicated comfort measures and sedation are effectively carried out.

When competent terminal patients elect to shorten suffering at the end of life by voluntarily refusing hydration, they must be able to participate in medical decision making and make an informed and voluntary choice in favor of the option. They must elect to forgo all forms of oral and intravenous fluid intake other than the tiny amounts necessary to deliver medications, and they must understand that the withholding of fluids is to be complete and is to continue until the time of death, unless they reverse the decision early in the process while still able to do so. This understanding is mutually developed by both the patient and the physician as a rational medical decision that is documented in the medical record.

Concurrently, the physician and nurses must agree to see the process through to the end, and they must act to prevent any symptoms of distress the patient may experience. For symptoms that might be arising from the basic fatal disease itself, there is a spectrum of medication that can be appropriate. Pain medication is continued as necessary, and for agitation and/or anxiety, antianxiety medications are effective. When heavy duty sedation is required in order to bring about a peaceful state, the barbiturates are available. They can be used intravenously in a continuous, concentrated, slow infusion to provide the desired state of unawareness. This is done in a dose sufficient to relieve all distress with the dose being increased until the patient is asleep and peaceful—a procedure described as terminal sedation.

Two barbiturates can be used. Pentobarbital sodium (Nembutal) solution is rapid in onset and short in duration. Thiopental sodium (Pentothal) is an ultra-fast-acting barbiturate that has been used extensively for short, general anesthesia or for the induction of anesthesia. The effects of both these drugs can be sustained by continuous infusion under the direction of the physician. By concentrating the drug in a very small amount of fluid, the desired dehydration is not significantly interrupted. Specific details of this procedure have been described for physicians,[11] and other standard references discuss the pharmacology and preparation of these medications.[12] Propofol is another drug that is commonly used for prolonged sedation.[13]

In this situation, the physician is not constrained ethically by any particular maximum dose of the sedating drugs. The physician is able to use barbiturates in increasing doses, if needed, to the point of producing sleep and complete unconsciousness. The necessary amount of medication is administered continuously until the patient's death.

When using this option, the physician commits himself or herself to the use of these medications in sufficient doses and assures the patient and family of this commitment. However, this assurance, with which most physicians agree in principle, is often not carried into practice. In spite of the fact that it is now commonly agreed that ethically and legally the proper dose of medication for a patient at the end of life is that dose of medication that properly relieves the pain or distress, insufficient doses of medicine still are utilized all too often, either because of out-moded principles of pain therapy that are ingrained in the physician's reactions, or because of a simple lack of knowledge as to how to treat extreme distress.

Rob McStay wrote an important article on terminal sedation in 2003 in the *American Journal of Law and Medicine,* and he examines in detail the many legal and ethical aspects of this area of palliative medicine.[14] He defined *terminal sedation* as "the induction of an unconscious state to relieve otherwise intractable distress . . . frequently accompanied by the withdrawal of any life-sustaining intervention, such as hydration and nutrition. This practice is a clinical option of 'last resort' when less aggressive palliative care measures have failed. . . . Terminal sedation has been used for three related but distinct purposes: (1) to relieve physical pain; (2) to produce an unconscious state before the withdrawal of artificial life support; and (3) to relieve non-physical suffering." We can add a fourth purpose: to accompany voluntary refusal of all fluids in situations in which morphine-like drugs and anti-agitation medicines do not suffice to control distress. McStay reports that terminal sedation, according to several studies, usually results in death within two to four days.

In his concluding remarks, McStay states, "Terminal sedation is a legally justifiable practice, supported by established jurisprudence. The U.S. Supreme Court's tacit reliance on the existence of this practice is based upon long-standing principles arising from law and standards of clinical care." In McStay's opinion, "Criminal, civil and administrative penalties, whether related to a patient's death or to the prescription of controlled substances, are unwarranted. . . . As long as a practitioner . . . does not intend to cause or hasten death, the mere risk of death as a foreseeable consequence is not an unjustifiable risk, particularly with respect to end-of-life care."

Basis for Legality of Refusal of Fluids and Terminal Sedation

The primary legal issues involved in voluntary refusal of hydration revolve around the rights of terminally ill patients (1) to refuse hydration in order to end their suffering, and (2) to receive the medication necessary to relieve their suffering. As to the first right, virtually every American jurisdiction now recognizes the legal validity of refusing artificial nutrition and hydration, and competent adults now have the prerogative to refuse *any* form of unwanted treatment, regardless of the diagnosis and prognosis and of whether the patient is terminal or not. The state supreme court cases that established this right held that its exercise did not constitute suicide and that, under these circumstances, the removal of tubes providing nutrition and hydration did not constitute homicide or medical assistance in suicide.[15]

As to the second right to receive the medication necessary to relieve suffering, there appears to be general acceptance of the view that one commits neither homicide nor assistance in suicide if, as an incident of an otherwise medically appropriate plan of palliative treatment, one administers medication that reduces the duration of the dying process. Both elements of the procedure—the right to refuse forced hydration and the right to obtain effective medication for the treatment of distress—seem to have a claim to constitutional protection,[16] and in a growing number of jurisdictions, this acceptance is taking the form of legislation that explicitly codifies this legal position.[17]

This legal right to refuse any unwanted treatment, including hydration in all forms, is often not sufficiently appreciated by patients. I hope that the conscientious and informed physician, therefore, would discuss this when informing patients of their options. This sequence of patient-elected terminal dehydration brought on by refusal of hydration, accompanied by effective treatment of symptoms by medication (including terminal sedation when necessary), is underutilized as a means of assisting the dying because its legal basis is so poorly understood by patients and their physicians. Persons who have felt that the procedure meets their needs but whose doctors are not experienced in it (or object in some way) have had the option of asking for a consultation with or transfer to another physician who will consider this approach with you. It is a rightful option for the adult patient who is able to participate in medical decision making. Your doctor will be practicing according to accepted standards of good medical care if he or she helps you when you have elected voluntary withdrawal of all fluids. If you are not able to participate in decision making and have a properly appointed agent (proxy) for medical affairs, it also is the right of that agent to refuse hydration in your name.

The guidelines for making such decisions, discussed in the previous chapter, apply appropriately if you are participating in voluntarily refusing hydration.

PHYSICIAN AID-IN-DYING USING LETHAL DOSES OF BARBITURATES

The experience of friends of mine illustrates some of the reasons patients have used this method of hastening death.

I was not Jim's physician, but was a friend of his and his wife, Diane. I paid them a visit during the summer more than a decade ago, about a year after Jim's initial diagnosis of prostate cancer and surgery. When Diane ushered me onto the screened-in porch, Jim was in a comfortable chair and stood up to greet me, but with considerable effort. He moved very slowly and from time to time winced with evident pain in his back. Jim steered conversation immediately to the great problems he was having with pain and weakness—ending life at a time of his choosing was on his mind.

He told me, "What is ahead is a lot more pain, and it's going to take a lot of that pain killer to make it bearable. I'll be a zombie. And I'm already weak as a pup—more so every day." Jim feared losing control of his life. His horizons had already been constricted to the porch and the adjacent living room where a hospital bed had been installed.

Ten years later, Jim's widow, Diane, was going over her husband's death with me after I had asked her if we could talk about this again. "Jim was so straightforward about it, so open about what he wanted. He and I had had a good understanding about life and its problems, and neither of us was going to go behind the other's back." This was true, she said, when that last, final problem arose—prostate cancer.

As often happens when prostate cancer occurs in a relatively young man (he was in his fifties at the time), the malignancy was aggressive in nature. He had had a prostatectomy and subsequent hormone treatment, but only five months after the initial surgery, discouraging evidence appeared that the growth had spread. Diane recalled, "At the time of the surgery, he had a positive outlook, but soon it was clear he was not going to make it. The cancer invaded his body too much and was in his bones. It was beginning to cause a lot of pain."

Diane told me that Jim's response to his situation was influenced tremendously by the sort of person he had been. "He had had a life he wanted and was a take-charge person. He was not controlling, but was very clear about what he wanted and did not want at the end of his life. He didn't want to be helpless." She said that being incapacitated and weak was anathema to Jim, and he wanted to die soon while he was still relatively peaceful and in control. He and Diane had talked things over carefully. Having drawn up a living will and signed a medical proxy statement, he gave his wife the legal authority to speak for him if he became unable to speak for himself.

Diane said that Jim's wish to end his life was not just a matter of pain control. Pain management could be dealt with fairly well. Jim was getting regular visits from hospice, and he had various comfort measures, support from the family, and supervision of his pain medication. He was receiving good amounts of major narcotics to relieve the pain, and not long after our visit, he went to a continuous intravenous morphine drip that took away most of the pain. So, it was more than the pain itself. The amount of medication required left him feeling totally without energy and somnolent, and he became almost unable to get out of bed. This was what he dreaded—losing control and being forced into indignity. He wanted to choose how he died, and not the least of his wishes was to spare his wife and family a prolonged ordeal. As Diane described this, tears came to her eyes, even ten years after the fact. She loved Jim then and still does. "You know, even now I seem to miss him more each year."

Diane said that some weeks after I had made my visit to Jim that last summer of his life, he had accumulated a supply of Seconal sufficient to end his life, and he had chosen a date on which he would take the capsules. Their grown-up children and a physician nephew, Scott, were informed and were asked to be present. Watching Jim go through his final weeks had been painful for all of them, but they understood what he wanted and did not disagree with his wish.

Diane described the last day. "Jim took the medication in the early evening. We were all there. He started swallowing pills as quickly as he could, but it was slow going and after only several minutes he said, 'I can't take any more.' I'm not sure how many he took, but within five minutes he was asleep." Diane said, "After an hour or so, I didn't think it was going to work, so I went to the other room. He had not taken enough of the pills."

However, Jim, watched by his physician nephew, remained completely unconscious. Diane recalled that Jim's breathing became somewhat noisy after an hour or so, which must have been due to his not clearing airway secretions—but there was no distress on his part. He was unaware of anything. His breathing and heart action stopped in the early morning hours, and Diane described all of the family gathering around. They decided not to call Jim's doctor at 2:00 AM, and all went to bed except for Scott who remained in the room with Jim until morning came. Diane did not sleep, but said she felt relieved. "We all did."

When morning came, the doctor was called and came to the house at around 7:00 AM. He filled out the death certificate, certifying that Jim had died from metastatic cancer of the prostate as the underlying disease—which was true. Diane related that later that day the children went through all the family pictures and made a collage of Jim's life. They were at peace with what happened. Except for being somewhat drawn out for the family and seeming at one point to Diane and Scott not to be working, Jim's death was the death he had wanted. For him the distress and suffering were over after the first five minutes.

"Was there anything you would have done differently?" I asked Diane.

"No. It's about choice and respecting Jim's choice. It's really about him."

Characteristics of Seconal and Nembutal

Ten to twenty years ago most doctors, if they gave a patient in Jim's situation prescriptions for Seconal or Nembutal, would have made the total dose six grams, usually prescribed in multiple prescriptions that added up to the total desired, and usually accumulated by the patient over a period of time. If this happened in the last few years, Jim would have been given a larger dose (nine or ten grams) and his death would have occurred more quickly. Doctors have found that no one who takes and retains that dose lives beyond twenty-four hours, and most will die in the first hour. Another action that would be different if this approach were used now would be that the barbiturate capsules would be pulled or cut apart and the powder emptied into a few tablespoons of applesauce or some fruit juice. Physicians who have assisted patients in this way have found that the medication is more easily and rapidly ingested as a powder mixed in a vehicle, such as applesauce or juice, rather than as many individual capsules, or the barbiturate might be obtained in a liquid form which can be drunk readily (although bitter).

In 1991, Derek Humphry published a landmark book, *Final Exit*,[18] which described in detail how a terminal, suffering patient might end his life with barbiturates. The book, a best seller, did a tremendous amount to bring this option to the public's attention. The use of barbiturates for this purpose is outlined in the 2002 third edition of that book[19] and by authorities in Oregon,[20] the one state in this country in which such practice is legal. (See Appendix B.) Physicians in Oregon have commonly used Seconal (secobarbital) and Nembutal (pentobarbital) for this purpose. These capsules are made in 50- and 100-milligram sizes containing the drug as a powder, which is a normal dose for treating insomnia (for which they are practically never used anymore). Pentobarbital can also be obtained in a liquid form in Oregon.

It is well established now that a lethal dose of these two barbiturates is nine grams (90 capsules of 100 milligrams each), but in the last several years many physicians have used ten grams. The Fifth Annual Report on Oregon's Death with Dignity Act indicates that when ten grams of pentobarbital is used, half of all patients died within fifteen minutes. The ten-gram dose is probably now being used most often. However, nine grams is certainly lethal, albeit the median time of dying is slightly longer (thirty to sixty minutes).[21] Doctors have advised that the entire dose be taken within a minute or two since the patient needs to get the entire amount ingested before going to sleep, which occurs very promptly. As noted previously, mixing the powder in applesauce quickens ingestion. In addition to the barbiturate, certain adjunctive (helper) medicines have been used by doctors to facilitate the action of the drug.[22]

Although the dose of nine or ten grams of secobarbital or pentobarbital has been generally regarded as being definitely lethal in all instances, early in 2005 one person took such a dose and did not die. This is the only failure of which end-of-life advocates are aware, both in this country and in Europe. That person's attempt at ending his life was observed by competent observers who are clear that he took the entire dose and did not vomit it. The reason for this one exception is not certain but is thought to be related to his having been on another medication that interfered with the absorption of the barbiturate from the intestinal tract.

The shelf life of barbiturates has been a question in the minds of persons who have stockpiled the medication for later use. It is hard to have a dogmatic answer to this question since the expiration date of most medications is a conservative one recommended by the manufacturers (and rightly so). It is probable that many drugs may retain their potency to a large extent beyond the expiration date, or, if there is a reduction in potency, it is a gradual loss over time—but one cannot assure this. I am aware of anecdotal evidence from a number of my colleagues that if a barbiturate is stored in a dry environment at room temperature (not in the refrigerator), it probably retains potency for a few years (maybe five or seven), which I purposely do not define more explicitly because it is impossible to do so with accuracy. It can be said, however, that these barbiturates are generally fairly stable compounds that deteriorate in effectiveness quite slowly. Some persons have used a larger dose if they felt the potency was reduced.

Legality of Barbiturate Use

If you live in Oregon, the barbiturate can be legally obtained through your physician (as of the writing of this chapter). In other states, in the past a lethal dose could be secured only by obtaining small amounts of the drug over a period of time from multiple prescriptions, ostensibly for the problem of insomnia. The drug would be gradually stockpiled until a lethal dose was attained. (At present, even with a prescription, such drugs are hard to obtain—see the following text.)

Ending one's life is generally thought not to be a crime, but assisting someone to end his or her life may put one in legal jeopardy, depending on the state involved. At the present time in the United States, the physician's prescribing of medication for the purpose of ending life under carefully described circumstances is clearly legal in the state of Oregon (see Appendix B), but outside Oregon, the situation is difficult. In some states, there is simply no statute covering the situation; in others the legality of the action may be in a gray zone. This means that the physician and others who assist in suicide may run legal risks if the action is discovered. The amount of this risk depends on the specific laws of the various states,[23] the attitudes of local prosecutors, and the attitudes of other people in the family or circle of friends who may become privy to the event. For this reason, most physicians who have written prescriptions for this purpose have felt that the fewer people who are aware of what is happening, the better—and then only those persons who are in complete sympathy with the planned action. It is fortunate that most of the time a spouse, grown child, or friend has not wished these actions to be known by others to preserve family privacy and patient dignity. A better situation will exist in the future when such actions are clearly legal as a form of end-of-life treatment, and there is no need to have any concerns about the event being more widely known.

Simply being present in the room observing the act has not been regarded by most as "assisting in suicide," but family and friends should be aware that this is poorly defined. At the present time, the patient must physically perform the act of taking the medication himself or herself, unassisted. *Final Exit* provides explicit details about these considerations and other details for setting up a planned death.

In Canada, the laws regarding assisting in suicide are stricter than in this country, and the definition of assisting in suicide may be broader than in the United States. In November 2004, a seventy-three-year-old Canadian woman, Evelyn Martens, who had been charged with physically assisting two persons in suicide, was acquitted by a jury, but only after many months of preliminary investigation and legal process by the Canadian legal system. This is chilling, even though it occurred in Canada and not in this country, and there are a few similar cases pending in other countries.

Availability of Barbiturates

If a patient outside Oregon wishes to obtain barbiturates, there are real obstacles. First, there is the problem of availability of the medication from the manufacturers and distributors of Seconal and Nembutal. Even with a prescription, the drugs are becoming exceedingly difficult to obtain. Many drugstores do not carry the medications since their main use now is for hastening death in terminal illness, and drugstore records are increasingly scrutinized by regulatory authorities who look for illegal use. Not only are the medications often not stocked in a pharmacy, they are often not available from wholesale distributors. One of the major pharmaceutical companies that used to manufacture Seconal, Eli Lilly, no longer does so, citing an insufficient market for the drug.[24] However, as of 2004, another company has begun producing and supplying Seconal again (Ranbaxy).

Another recent, major potential difficulty in obtaining barbiturates was that John Ashcroft, the former U. S. Attorney General, late in 2001 issued a directive to Drug Enforcement Agency staff that physicians' prescribing of barbiturates for the purpose of hastening death is to be considered illegal by federal regulation. The case finally ended in January 2006 when the U.S. Supreme Court held in a 6–3 decision that the Attorney General had overstepped his authority.

Veterinary sources were helpful for a few years, but are now less available. Sources abroad have been utilized successfully sometimes, but it is difficult for an individual patient to know where to turn. Street sources have also been used, but these have been dangerous because of the unreliability of the source. Google on the Internet has produced a large number of sites that have information about the drugs, but again, one does not know exactly with whom one is working. Patients who have been successful in obtaining the drugs have done so by asking their own doctors or others in their own local medical community, or by discussing the problem with contacts in the end-of-life advocacy movement (see Appendix A). There has been no one way.

A patient might feel that in view of all the difficulty, some other medication might be used, one that is more easily available. However, there has been no other class of medication that has had the speed and certainty of result that the barbiturates have had when taken in a lethal dose. Many different substances have been used over the years in suicide attempts (apart from end of life), and the results of these attempts vary tremendously. Few persons wishing to hasten death in the setting of unrelieved suffering at the end of life have wanted to risk any uncertainty.

DRAWBACKS TO SECRECY

If you live outside Oregon and your doctor cannot legally participate in hastening death by prescribing barbiturates, he or she will either refuse to help or will invoke secrecy, hoping to avoid legal risk as much as possible. Even though this works most of the time, the secrecy approach has some very real drawbacks:

1. Consultation with other doctors is usually reduced, and the potential disadvantages of this are obvious.
2. Anything having to do with the actual act of arranging for the barbiturate's purchase, preparation, and administration—or with the justification for the use thereof—is necessarily more difficult under conditions of secrecy.

3. There is palpable anxiety when the doctor, patient, or family members know that anticipated actions can possibly result in legal charges of assisting in suicide. If the circle of those who know about barbiturate use is kept small and is limited to only those persons who are in favor of helping the patient with this option, the secrecy is likely to prevail, in which case there are no undesired consequences. However, this is hard to guarantee. The risk may be almost nil in jurisdictions where there is not an aggressive prosecutor or where the state laws are vague, but there is always some degree of anxiety and persisting fear of legal jeopardy that attends secrecy.

4. If secrecy were attempted in a case brought to the prosecutor's attention in the context of possible legal misconduct, the mere fact that secrecy had been attempted might be a plus for prosecutors. They might ask, "If you are trying to defend your action as proper, why did you attempt to hide your action?"

Most of my colleagues who sign death certificates in this situation cite the basic underlying disease as the cause of death, not citing an intentional overdose of a barbiturate (except in Oregon where the physician can be open about what happened). The medical examiner has not been involved most of the time since the patient has had a terminal illness and has been expected to die soon in any event—a situation the patient's physician normally handled without notifying the medical examiner. Although this is often done (outside Oregon), it is a form of secrecy to the extent that the role of barbiturates is not acknowledged. It is a less than ideal situation when the physician cannot be completely open about what is going on. Even without legislation that clearly gives protection to the physician, these legal risks are low, but they are not completely absent. Physicians will vary in their willingness to assist in hastening death when they do not have such legal protection.

The use of barbiturates to hasten death in situations of intolerable suffering has many associated problems for persons other than Oregonians. The next means of hastening death (described in the following chapter on the use of helium) has dealt with many of these problems because the action can be carried out by the patient without physician assistance or the need for prescriptions.

9

HELIUM: NEWLY USED METHOD
TO END SUFFERING

Patient autonomy at the end of life has been advanced by a new method of hastening death, the use of helium. In 2000 and the years preceding, barbiturates were the most commonly used means for a planned death, but, as we have seen in the last several years, obtaining barbiturates has become so difficult that the use of helium in this country has arisen as an alternative to be considered.

In this chapter, I report how some persons have used helium to relieve intolerable suffering when all else has failed (as similarly in the preceding chapter I have discussed the use of barbiturates for the same purpose). I stress that this is reporting about how these options have been used in such circumstances, and it is not advice. My reporting of what some patients do when facing a bad death simply indicates that ending their life is an option they have felt compelled to consider when making their decisions as to how to cope.

When helium—an odorless, nonflammable and nonexplosive gas—is used, a prompt, easy, and almost certain death has been obtained by terminal patients who have been suffering intolerably and have wished to hasten their deaths. In my discussions with end-of-life rights advocates who have been aware of the details of the use of helium for this purpose, I have learned of extremely few failures, unpleasant symptoms, or unexpected outcomes (one exception I shall discuss later in this chapter). Unconsciousness occurs within forty-five to sixty seconds, and all patients' hearts stop within fifteen minutes, usually sooner.[1]

At the time this chapter was written, the medical literature had few reports on the use of helium for planned death, but Russel Ogden in the Department of Criminology, Kwantlen University College, New Westminster, British Columbia, Canada, published a single case report of a death associated with breathing helium. He felt this was the first published report of this sort of death.[2] There are a handful of other case reports since his article, but I have been unable to find an article in a major medical journal that reviews the topic and all known deaths from this cause. However, Derek Humphry has described the use of helium in detail in the third edition of his well-known book *Final Exit* and in a 2006 video of the same name.[3] An Internet search of the Web produces quite a few sites that discuss the topic, but most of these are anecdotal and not of the quality a peer-reviewed medical journal would have, although Faye Girsh did produce a very good discussion on the Internet, "The Many Ways to Hasten Death," which included helium.[4]

Physiology of the Use of Helium at End of Life

A word about the physiology involved will help in understanding how the helium method works. The use of 100 percent helium brings about death by depriving the brain of oxygen. Normally, when one breathes air into the lungs, 20.9 percent of the room air breathed in is oxygen, which is essential to most basic functions of the body. (In addition to oxygen, ordinary air consists of 78.1 percent nitrogen, 0.036 percent carbon dioxide and a few other gases in trace amounts.) If one is deprived of all oxygen, consciousness is lost in less than one minute. This oxygen lack is not associated with any unpleasant sensation.

If one were to be smothered or otherwise suffocated, air hunger and frightening distress would develop. However, this distress is due not to oxygen deprivation, but to the buildup of carbon dioxide in the body, since the carbon dioxide is not exhaled. (Carbon dioxide is a normal waste product that is disposed of through the lungs with each breath.) Excess carbon dioxide causes one to feel the need to breathe more rapidly and deeply (air hunger). With the acute onset of a severe lack of oxygen alone—in the absence of carbon dioxide buildup—one simply drifts off into unconsciousness due to the reduced oxygen levels in the blood, and there is no sensation of air hunger since there is no time for carbon dioxide to build up in the body.

I have personally experienced oxygen lack and can attest to the absence of any distress. When I was in the Air Force as a flight surgeon in the 1950s, I went through physiology training in a high-altitude chamber at Randolph Air Force Base in Texas. A group of us were in the chamber at a simulated altitude of 43,000 feet, at which altitude the atmospheric pressure is extremely reduced and the concentration of oxygen extremely low. One can maintain consciousness only by breathing oxygen from a pressurized mask. (In an airplane at that high altitude, the cabin is pressurized with air that allows sufficient oxygen to be inhaled without the special pressurized masks we were wearing.) The instructor said that taking off the mask at that simulated altitude would result in passing out in a matter of seconds, due to a lack of oxygen. He asked that one of us demonstrate the effects of insufficient oxygen by taking off his mask and at the same moment begin writing his name on a pad. He promised he would be by the side of the volunteer to reapply the mask immediately when needed. For some reason that now escapes me, I volunteered. I wrote my name normally once, but before I could write it a second time my handwriting degenerated into a scrawl due to a lack of oxygen, at which point the mask was put back on me. There had been absolutely no unpleasant sensation because I had been able to continue to breathe off carbon dioxide with each exhalation—I just was not getting sufficient oxygen from my inhalations of the thin air in the low pressure chamber. There was certainly no air hunger or feeling of suffocation.

The same thing that happened to me in the altitude chamber will happen to any person who breathes 100 percent helium or other inert gases (e.g., pure nitrogen) from a small plastic tent over the head.

Helium Has Been Used to End Suffering[5]

Anyone can obtain helium by going to one of the chain discount or toy stores for 100 percent helium that is sold in tanks for the purpose of inflating party balloons. The cost of a small tank is around $30. People who have used helium to end life have bought two tanks to be certain enough is on hand, a point that has been stressed by persons with firsthand knowledge of such patients. Often a plastic T-tube has been used to run helium simultaneously from the two tanks into the plastic tent that is used as a hood, although many persons have used a single tube, with the second tank being held in reserve in case it is needed. The plastic tubing used to convey the helium from the tank to the hood has been obtained in hardware stores, but there are sources from which a manufactured kit can be obtained, helping assure that connections fit properly.

As can be seen in Derek Humphry's video (and as I learn from colleagues of mine who have observed end-of-life events using helium), when the collapsed small tent has been prepositioned at the forehead level and the helium has been turned on, the tent distends with helium, displacing the air (and oxygen). The tent stands upright, lifted like a balloon by the lighter-than-air helium. If the patient draws it down over the head and secures it loosely around the neck by a soft elastic band or a Velcro fastener, he or she will begin at that point to breathe in the helium contained in the tent. Consciousness is rapidly lost due to a lack of oxygen, as noted previously, and within a very few minutes the heart stops, and breathing ceases. Afterward, an observer/friend has usually disposed of the tubing, tank, and plastic tent, as Derek Humphry has written and portrayed.

Build-up of carbon dioxide (and consequent air hunger) does not occur because there is insufficient time for the carbon dioxide to accumulate significantly, either in the tent or in the blood stream. In the past, plastic bags without helium have been used to end life, and in that instance air hunger can be noted by the patient because the process is not nearly as fast as with 100 percent helium.

Helium has been used to end a suffering patient's terminal illness probably more than two hundred times in this country with rare difficulty. The only exceptions apparently have been a handful of instances in which there was imprecise matching of tubing at connecting points, such that some room air got into the bag in a quantity that interfered with the action of the helium. This has not happened in situations in which all connections are secure.

The families of patients who have ended their suffering in this manner have usually called hospice or the personal physician to report that the patient has stopped breathing. Many families have delayed the reporting of the death for an hour or two to ensure that, if 911 emergency services become involved, it will be absolutely clear that the patient has died. When the family physician or a hospice worker has pronounced the patient dead, the funeral director has been notified and has come to the scene. The funeral director generally then has the physician or hospice worker sign the death certificate, which indicates the underlying terminal disease as the cause of death. The family that abides by the wishes of the dying patient would not call 911 since the patient would not have wanted to summon resuscitative resources. (The problems of calling 911 when one does not wish for resuscitative efforts are discussed in Chapter 12, on medical planning.)

A Patient with Lou Gehrig's Disease Uses Helium

Ethel, a patient in her fifties of one of my colleagues, used helium to end her life. She had Lou Gehrig's disease, a universally fatal condition known as amyotrophic lateral sclerosis (ALS). Ethel and Ron, her ex-husband, had divorced before the end of her life approached, but they were still close friends. Ron and their four children were very supportive of Ethel's fight against this disease and her ultimate decision to hasten her dying process.

As her disease progressed, Ethel lost use of her legs and was confined to a wheelchair. Her arms became steadily weaker, and it was only a short time before she would become completely helpless. Her death would probably be caused by respiratory failure due to her increasingly weakening muscles, which no longer would be able to support her breathing. Such a death was a bad prospect that Ethel decided she would meet on her own terms by planning her dying.

Ethel had heard that breathing 100 percent helium could bring about an extremely prompt, easy, and certain death, and she wanted this. She learned more about the method— filling a large plastic bag with helium and then pulling it down like a tent over the head. She learned that by breathing the helium from the bag, unconsciousness would ensue in less than a minute due to a lack of oxygen and that her heart would stop within a few minutes. With her decision made, Ethel bought a small tank of helium from a nearby store that sold the gas for use in party balloons. She also obtained a kit containing the proper tubing, plastic tent, and Velcro fasteners that would allow her easily to implement the procedure. She practiced the method except for turning on the helium valve and felt confident that breathing the helium would spare her the large amount of distress that loomed ahead for her.

Ethel lived at home in a big house. Two of her children lived nearby and were devotedly and frequently at hand to help her through her illness. On the day before she planned to end her life, all her children and her former husband were present. Then, and in the preceding week, there had been favorite stories and reminiscences of good times in the past. A volunteer had seen her again that day, and in the evening a physician also met with her and talked about how death would occur and what would happen, were she to elect to go ahead with her plan. The physician's presence was psychologically helpful to both Ethel and her family, and they were relatively at ease.

On the next day, which she had selected as the day of her death, Ethel was in her bedroom, propped up in bed, surrounded by her family. Two of the children sat on the bed on either side of her. Although very weak, she was able by herself to turn the valve that filled the tent with helium and then to draw it down over her head. Ethel died very quickly—and her death was remarkably peaceful.

The family, wishing for some private time, waited two hours, and then notified the local hospice that Ethel had died (she had been in hospice care for several months). A "declarer" with legal authority to pronounce death in hospice patients came to the home to do so. The use of helium was not discussed with the hospice personnel, and it was presumed that the patient had simply died of her disease. (The family had taken away all equipment related to the helium so there was no physical evidence of its use). The hospice worker signed the official death certificate, and the undertaker was notified. Ethel's death was entirely what she and the family had wanted—fast, certain, and free of distress—and she had remained in control.

Advantages of Helium

Many doctors have found that the use of helium is now the speediest and most available method (outside Oregon) for a patient in this country to end life when faced with intolerable suffering. Helium has had some definite advantages over the use of barbiturates because it is far faster, it is easy to use, and the helium—at least presently—is easily available. Like a lethal dose of barbiturates, it also has been certain.

With regard to legal liability, as far as I have learned, there has so far been no legal action taken anywhere in this country against a bystander or family member when the patient has used this method to end life. The patient without any physical help from those in attendance has carried out the administration of the helium by turning on the helium that fills the bag-like tent and then pulling the tent down over the head, unassisted.

The use of helium can be carried out without the assistance or even the knowledge of the physician. It does not require any prescription writing on the part of the physician, this being a plus, since many physicians outside Oregon, fearing liability, do not wish to write prescriptions for barbiturates in this situation. (On the other hand, nonparticipation by the personal physician deprives the patient and family of the important emotional and psychological support that derives from the moral assistance of the doctor.) It is also a method that can be accomplished by patients themselves. The tubing has been relatively easy to purchase by mail, something the patient could do. Presumably, some of the patients have had family members or friends who have driven them to the store to get the helium tank, but still it has been regarded as an action of the patient, which has been essential in order for bystanders (family, friends, or members of a right-to-die organization) to stay on the right side of the law. If the patient were in a nursing home or other medical facility, it would be much harder to make this event come about purely by the efforts of the patient—a probably insurmountable drawback.

In localities in which the state law or the stance of law enforcement officials is averse to the use of barbiturates, or in which the necessary amount of barbiturates is very difficult to obtain, helium has been found to be an alternative. There also continues to be active research into other somewhat similar means of oxygen deprivation.

DIFFERENTIATING SADNESS AT THE END OF LIFE FROM CLINICAL DEPRESSION

When a terminally ill patient with less than six months to live decides to hasten death because of intolerable suffering despite meticulous comfort care, it is not the same as a depressed patient becoming suicidal. Typically, the word *suicidal* is used for patients whose *psychiatric* conditions make them temporarily and irrationally want to end their lives because of acute psychological distress. By contrast, the term *hastening death* is more appropriate for patients whose *medical* conditions are terminal and who make a rational choice to shorten the dying process by days or weeks to avoid intolerable suffering. Understanding the difference between suicidal depression and hastening an imminent death is essential to protecting the right of terminally ill patients to remain in control and choose the manner of their death while at the same time protecting vulnerable psychiatric patients whose safety needs to be ensured. If you or a family member are terminally ill, understanding this distinction may also be key to defending against any suggestion that refusing unwanted medical treatment or wishing to hasten death is tantamount to being suicidally depressed when it is simply making a rational end-of-life choice.

REVISITING DAVID'S CASE

In Chapter 7 on hastening death, we discussed the case of David who in his early sixties developed a recurrence of cancer at the back of his tongue. Further treatment with surgery, radiation, or chemotherapy was not possible at the time. Given the location of David's cancer, as the tumor grew he faced severe anxiety and agitation as his ability to breathe became compromised. Even meticulous comfort care and pain management could not prevent a bad death in David's case.

When David made the decision to hasten his death, he experienced considerable relief. David was appropriately sad facing the end of life, but he felt grateful for the extra years he had had after earlier aggressive medical treatment for his cancer had twice restored him to reasonable health. Would he have liked to have that option available to him again? Of course. But he accepted with dignity that this was no longer the case.

After David's recurrence was diagnosed, he experienced some apprehension and difficulty sleeping in the weeks before he broached with his wife Abigail and me the possible hastening of his death. Once he had brought his plan of a barbiturate overdose into the open, however, he felt overwhelmingly relieved. David knew he had made the right choice for himself.

Mark's Suicidal Depression

In contrast to David, Mark was a young man in his thirties who became severely depressed when his fiancée Carolyn was killed in a tragic car accident just months before they were to be married. Mark and Carolyn had dated for five years and had been engaged for two. Mark simply could not imagine life without Carolyn. The senselessness of her death (she was killed by a drunken driver) was overwhelming.

As Mark sank into a morbid depression, he developed insomnia, lacked appetite, dropped fifteen pounds, lost all interest in work or pleasure, and finally became suicidal. As the date of what would have been his wedding approached, Mark's family and friends became alarmed as he expressed thoughts of joining Carolyn by committing suicide. Finally, Mark's family brought him to an emergency room where he was hospitalized against his will in a psychiatric ward to ensure his safety.

Fortunately, Mark responded well to a combination of psychotherapy and antidepressant medication. Once he was no longer depressed, his suicidal thoughts were in his words "unfathomable" and an "irrational reaction to Carolyn's death." Mark resumed his career as a computer programmer, eventually began dating, and married another woman. He ultimately came to feel that was what Carolyn would have wanted him to do. Certainly, he would have wanted Carolyn to move on with her life had their fates been reversed.

Note the contrasts between David's case and Mark's. David was terminally ill with recurrent cancer of the tongue for which no treatment was available to restore his health, and he faced a gruesome death in a matter of weeks. David was dying, not living. He made a rational choice to shorten his death under the circumstances.

By contrast, Mark was in excellent physical health. He had a long, satisfying life to look forward to if he could overcome his depression over Carolyn's death. His suicidal thoughts were an irrational escape from his acute psychological distress. Whereas David needed his family and doctor to support hastening his death, Mark needed his family and doctors to ensure his safety at a time when he could not.

SYMPTOMS OF DEPRESSION VERSUS TERMINAL ILLNESS

Depression can be thought of as having both psychological and physical symptoms. The psychological symptoms include feeling helpless, hopeless, and worthless. The physical symptoms can include insomnia, lethargy, lack of appetite, and weight loss. In general, as patients become more severely depressed, they develop more severe physical symptoms of depression and have increasing difficulty functioning. A mildly depressed patient may feel depressed but have minimal physical symptoms of depression and be functioning fine, but a severely depressed patient like Mark may have severe physical symptoms (severe insomnia, weight loss, and fatigue) and be unable to function.

The American Psychiatric Association has identified nine symptoms of depression:[1]

1. Depressed mood for at least two weeks
2. Markedly diminished interest or pleasure in activities
3. Significant weight loss or weight gain
4. Insomnia or oversleeping
5. Agitation or listlessness
6. Fatigue or loss of energy
7. Feelings of worthlessness or excessive, inappropriate guilt
8. Diminished ability to think or concentrate, or indecisiveness
9. Recurrent thoughts of death or suicide

Note that the physical symptoms of depression can also be caused by terminal medical conditions. For example, fatigue, difficulty sleeping, lack of appetite, and weight loss can all be symptoms of many cancers. If a terminal patient's physical symptoms can be accounted for by his medical illness, they should not be counted toward a diagnosis of depression, according to the American Psychiatric Association guidelines for diagnosing depression.[2]

In terms of psychological (as opposed to physical) symptoms of depression, the psychological core of depression is paralysis and self-recrimination, rather than genuine sadness. Genuine sadness is cathartic and empowering in contrast to depression, which is paralyzing and self-reproaching. Mark felt helpless, hopeless, and worthless in his suicidal depression. By contrast, David felt appropriately sad and empowered in his decision to hasten his death.

Suicidal thoughts can occur not just in depression but in other psychiatric conditions as well. The same general principles apply.

HASTENING DEATH VERSUS SUICIDAL DEPRESSION

When patients are not suicidal but instead are making a reasonable choice to hasten death, all of the following criteria are met. The patient is:

- Terminally ill with a medical illness
- Expected to die imminently, within six months
- Suffering intolerably due to symptoms of the medical condition despite meticulous comfort care
- Making a rational choice to shorten the dying process under these unusual circumstances

By contrast, when a psychiatric patient is suicidal, the above criteria cannot all be met.

If you or a family member is having difficulty differentiating the desire to hasten death in the face of suffering at the end of life from what we normally think of as the desire to commit suicide, you can always consult with a psychiatrist. But, be sure to consult with a psychiatrist empathetic to the possibility of hastening death in terminal illness. If your decision to hasten death meets all of the criteria set forth in Chapter 7 on hastening death and you feel confident of your decision, your appropriate sadness should not be mislabeled depression. Nor should unwanted psychotherapy and/or antidepressant medication be pressed upon you.

Ending life in a rational decision not driven by psychiatric illness becomes more difficult when the problem is not terminal (defined as six months or less to live), but rather is a nonterminal condition of unrelieved suffering or distress, such as can occur in persons with oncoming dementia, infirmity and dependence on dialysis, certain cases of quadriplegia, totally disabling Parkinsonism, and other similar progressive or persistent disorders. There is no easy answer or obvious guideline for such a person, but clearly instances occur in which it could be rational to wish for the end of life in a nonterminal situation.

The Special Case of Irreversible Dementia and End-of-Life Management

❧

Most of us have a very real fear of being incapacitated mentally while our bodies continue to function reasonably well—the situation that can so often go on for years in Alzheimer's disease or other forms of dementia. One of my colleagues wrote me of his wife's mother and the trap she fell into because of this disease.

> My first experience with what was called "Alzheimer's" was the worst. My first wife's mother [Susan] . . . was institutionalized with it at a fairly early age, in her 60s I think. . . . [Susan had] feared it all her life since her own mother had had dementia. [Susan] was an absolutely brilliant and very refined woman. She was very concerned with appearances. Every time she had difficulty remembering a word or forgot a task, she worried it was the onset of what her mother had had.
>
> Tragically, she ended up gradually losing her memory and her grip on what was going on around her. Ultimately, [her husband] . . . had her institutionalized. My wife and I visited [Susan] . . . at the institution over the several years she was there, and it was a horror for my wife and me.
>
> In the end, she was like a restless, pained animal—sitting in a chair pulling against her restraints. I kept hoping that

she had no lucid moments, and I always thought how terrible she would have felt had she ever been able to foresee how she would actually spend her last years!

Few want to live in a state of being unable to recognize friends and family, know who one is or has been, know where one is, care for oneself personally, or interact with one's surroundings in any way intellectually. Adding to this fear is the fact that present guidelines for decision making at the end of life are insufficient in patients with Alzheimer's disease and other irreversible dementias. The dilemma is that there are no secure and dependable means for ensuring that in the future one's wishes for care, developed while competent, will be followed when dementia supervenes. If someone acts to end life while still mentally capable of doing so, this can result in a death that is premature. There is no obvious or easy answer.

Attempts have been made to propose workable rules for making decisions in this situation, but usually efforts are frustrated. A group of my colleagues and I met four times in Boston during 2005 in an effort to work out some reasonable guidelines, and, although we were able to agree on a number of points, there were many difficulties.[1]

What many of us would like is to ensure that, if in the future we become demented, we do not continue to live. It is very hard to ensure this wish can be met. We need to be able to put into place a precommitment by the present self that will override the possibility that the future incompetent self might countermand the directions set forth by the previously competent self.[2] Such prospective guidelines for shortening the period of dementia may be rejected by the future incompetent person. If the patient waits until dementia has occurred, he or she is, by definition, at that time unable to prescribe desired rules for care. Additionally, if other persons exercise substituted decision making for the patient and such decisions hasten dying, there is the question: From whom did they get this authority?

There are, however, some measures that can make precommitments of a competent person more *likely* to be carried out when and if incompetence develops. Some of this, but not all, depends on needed changes of the law. In discussing the problem, I have used Alzheimer's disease as a model for all types of disabling dementia at the end of life since it is the most common cause. These suggestions can apply to all the various forms of irreversible dementia.[3]

THE DILEMMA OF ALZHEIMER'S DISEASE

Alzheimer's disease is a progressive degeneration and loss of neurons in the brain, initially producing memory loss followed by steadily failing cognitive ability and dementia that severely affects behavior. Occurring equally in males and females over 65 (but sometimes earlier), the disease progresses to death in a course that can be prolonged over years. Microscopic tangles of neural fibers and plaques of an abnormal protein (amyloid) develop in most of the cortex and some of the subcortex of the brain, and certain other abnormal proteins can be detected in the diseased neurons. Diagnosis can be made with certainty only by autopsy, but because of the way the disease develops, certain blood tests and MRI imaging may also allow clinical diagnosis before death. Symptoms can range over a wide spectrum, and there is no typical case. Often, there is no reliable way to differentiate Alzheimer's disease from the various other conditions that may also produce dementia; vascular disease is the next most common cause of dementia. The incidence of Alzheimer's in both its symptomatic and asymptomatic forms is increasing (the latter diagnosed only by autopsy), and deaths from the disease are exceeded only by heart disease, cancer, and stroke. The Alzheimer Association, probably the biggest and most extensive advocacy group for families struggling to provide this care, is a good source of information about the disease.[4]

There is no known prevention for Alzheimer's disease—nor is there an effective treatment—and, discouragingly, the prospects for good medical answers in the near future are not great. Some experimental medications are being used, but their effectiveness to date has been very limited.

The costs of dementia are immense.[5] Dementia is associated with a tripling of Medicare expenditures, and financial costs for nursing home care in the United States for those with dementia are very high. The social cost is also vast—loss of dignity and suffering by the patient and family are incalculable. This continuation of physical life in the absence of sentient life imposes an incredible burden on our older population and their families. Since there is no good way to reverse the progress of Alzheimer's disease at present, many people have tried to think of ethical and legal means by which the suffering of Alzheimer's disease might be shortened.

WITHDRAWAL OF TREATMENTS THAT PROLONG LIFE: NOT A PROBLEM

As we have discussed earlier in this book, our society has slowly come to the universally held position that it is ethically and legally permissible to withhold or withdraw certain forms of treatment or support when a person who is competent refuses treatment or when an incompetent person has previously (when competent) given this authority to refuse to a proxy or agent by an advance directive.

Therefore, when treatment is withheld or withdrawn in the case of a patient with dementia *who has previously executed an advance directive along these lines*, there is unlikely to be justifiable protest, either legally or morally, and that person's life of mental incapacity can often be shortened by simply withholding these unwanted measures. If an advance directive has *not* been executed and the time for decision making about such treatments occurs after the patient has lost mental capacity, there still is not likely to be any legal problem, as long as there is agreement among the persons responsible for the person's care (relatives, a court-appointed guardian in the absence of relatives, and/or the responsible physician) that such a decision is in the best interests of the patient.

WITHHOLDING FOOD AND FLUIDS: MORE DIFFICULT

After rejecting unwanted treatments or procedures, the next move that comes to mind when a patient's advocate or agent is trying to shorten a period of suffering in a demented patient is to withhold food and fluid, thereby hastening the time of death. We have seen previously that in a *competent* person, this clearly is a right (terminal dehydration with sedation) since one cannot be forced to eat or drink.

This legal and ethical right, however, becomes more problematic when fluids are withheld from a *demented* person, even if that person has previously indicated to a proxy by written advance directive that he or she would not want to continue living under the circumstances of irreversible dementia and would prefer dying by withholding fluids. If the demented patient is thirsty and asks for or shows that he or she wants water, it would be nigh impossible for the agent or any caregiver to explain to the patient why he or she could not have water; sedation would have to be used to counter the patient's possible sense of distress. Directions to withhold fluids, given by the patient before becoming demented, could be challenged, even if they were strong and tightly written. Additional difficulty in withholding fluids from a demented person occurs if the patient appears to be contented and is not suffering in any way other than lacking cognitive function.

The problem is compounded further in the demented patient who has *not* executed such an advance directive or appointed a proxy. In such instance, there is no clear legal authority to carry out what the patient would have wanted. The caregiver is in a very gray area since the demented patient is likely to continue to want fluids and would have to be sedated in order to have such a course undertaken.

Assisted Suicide and Euthanasia in Dementia: Not Possible at Present

For the demented, assisted suicide and/or euthanasia are even more difficult procedures and are precluded by our current guidelines and laws. Even in Oregon, physician-assisted suicide is legally permissible only for *competent* patients who are terminally ill (and many demented patients are not terminally ill). The dilemma of incompetent patients is not addressed. Euthanasia is at present totally out of the picture legally.

What *Should* Be Possible, Ideally?

The demented patient by definition cannot commit suicide rationally, but while people are competent, they should be allowed to set forth in a legally binding document the circumstances under which they would wish, first, to have all fluids withheld (with the accompanying necessary sedation) so that death would intervene in a matter of days, or, second, to have a physician carry out active euthanasia with a lethal injection. The prior wishes of a competent self should be allowed to trump any possible later wishes of the confused, incompetent self. A change in the law would be necessary for this, but it is not far-fetched to picture legislatures allowing this at some time in the near future. The patient would have the right through such new legislation to define the circumstances of dementia under which he or she would not want to continue living. Withholding fluids and sedation is being done to some extent now in Europe, along with the even more aggressive remedy of active euthanasia for dementia under very carefully defined circumstances. We should do the same. With proper regulation there should be neither abuse nor a slippery slope.

A further reason for enacting legislation allowing the ending of a demented person's life in accordance with a predementia binding agreement is that it would avoid the pressure people who are worried about possible dementia might feel to end life prematurely. They could enjoy what rational life was left, if they knew a definite course of action was guaranteed prior to the onset of dementia. Otherwise, there is, as Ed Lowenstein, a member of our dementia discussion group, said, "the hazard that many will shorten their lives when not demented or while only very mildly demented because they are so determined to avoid life with serious dementia. They may be led to do this due to the recognition that dementia will rob them of the capability of hastening their own deaths."[6]

WHAT CAN BE DONE NOW, PRACTICALLY SPEAKING?

In the absence of new legislation, what can we do at the present time to avoid being kept alive indefinitely in a state of severe dementia? Taken together, the following suggestions, none of which is really new and none of which is guaranteed to lead to what each of us might ideally wish, probably will at least make an easier and more appropriate dying.

- Without fail, execute an advance directive that appoints an agent who is empathetic with one's wishes not to live into a life of dementia.
- Attach to the advance directive a supplementary detailed description of one's wishes, using as a model the special advance directive for dementia that is outlined in Appendix G. All these instructions might not be able to be carried out legally (in the absence of new legislation), but they can create a very clear picture of what one *wishes* and does *not* wish, such that the person appointed as agent clearly understands your wishes without any ambiguity.
- Specifically, make certain that the physician, all other caregivers, and the agent understand that without question you do not want to be transferred to a hospital, treated with antibiotics, intravenous or nasogastric feedings of fluids, or assisted in eating—or any treatment

other than comfort care measures only. This has all been discussed before, but avoidance of inappropriately prolonging life for the demented depends heavily on how vigorously the patient's advocates resist unwanted treatment or care. Too often, an advocate does not stand up firmly enough against the system because he or she is not convinced, or does not clearly understand, what is not wanted. Yet such resistance is perfectly legal at present. What is required is adamant determination on the part of the advocate.

- If you are a family member of a person with dementia, organize a conference that includes, as appropriate, family members, physician, social worker, nursing home supervisor, lawyer, and minister to discuss the patient's wishes and be sure that all are signed on to the agreed-upon approach. Note again that, even when there is no advance directive, if there is an agreement among family and caregivers as to the nature of treatment, there is virtually never any problem with actions (or nonactions) being challenged legally, when such actions are in the category of refusing unwanted measures.

- Make certain the goal of treatment and care for the patient is written down in the medical record. It should have been discussed at the conference noted previously, and this fact should be noted in the written record. Make clear that the goal is to shepherd the patient through the dying process, not to restore health.

- Make certain that all nursing home personnel are aware that family members expect the patient to die in the nursing home, not in a hospital. Their job will have been successful if the patient dies a peaceful death in the nursing home. Failure will occur if the patient is transferred out of the facility. They will do their job more effectively if they know this is the family's and agent's expectation, and there will be no fear on their part that they did not "do enough" (which can often be translated into inappropriate support and procedures).

- Work out an understanding with the caregivers that the patient will not be subjected to tests and diagnostic procedures, including such "routine" things as taking blood pressures and temperature readings. There is no need for these if the goal is to shorten the period of dementia. The only exception would be some measures needed for comfort care.

You will notice that these measures aimed at shortening the dying process in a demented patient have all been discussed earlier in the book in the context of the care any dying patient should have. The differences here are that in the demented patient, (1) these measures are often not undertaken because the patient is usually not dying or terminal and (2) the family and caregivers of a demented patient who is not terminal need to have heightened resolve not to prolong meaningless life since it is unusual to undertake these approaches in persons other than the terminally ill. Very firm determination is required.

Planning Ahead with Advance Directives: Staying in Control

❧❧❧

Planning Ahead Is Essential

Almost all the planning and legal aspects of medical care at the end of life have one underlying caveat: they must be done early if confusion, failure, and disappointment are to be avoided. Young persons often have a sense of invincibility that makes advance directives seem unimportant, and their usually good health provides no impetus. Older people may simply not get around to it or not realize the importance of such planning. However, regardless of one's age or state of health, advance planning is essential. When the unforeseen medical problem presents itself, everything will proceed more smoothly and with less angst when plans have been made ahead of time.

Advance Directives Usually Avoid the Need for Courts to Intervene

An advance directive is a written statement of how you wish to be cared for at the end of life. It is executed while you are competent and able to participate in medical decision-making. Written advance directives are the best and easiest means of avoiding situations in which it is not clear what you would have wanted, and they are extremely important in avoiding court-imposed directives that may go against your wishes. They should be executed by all adults who are intellectually competent to do so.

A majority of all the controversial end-of-life care problems that lead to court action occur when the patient is no longer able to make medical decisions and has not left clear-cut written evidence as to what he or she would have wanted. The courts generally do not wish to be involved in mandating what is to be done in such situations, but they are forced to be involved when there is family dissension and a lack of documented evidence of the patient's wishes. The Quinlan, Brody, and Schiavo cases are important court decisions in the history of end-of-life case law, but they (along with many other cases) never would have been necessary if proper advance directives had been in place.

The cases that appear on the front pages of newspapers are often about young people in desperate situations who cannot speak for themselves and have left no written evidence about their wishes for medical care. Every adult over the age of eighteen should have a properly executed advance directive. Older persons are more interested in advance directives since this age group has begun to contemplate the likelihood of disease and death in the relatively near future, but the young tend to feel that medical calamity will not befall them and do not plan ahead—sometimes with very bad consequences. Recently, I was giving a talk on end-of-life issues to a class of about seventy college students, and I asked for a show of hands by all who had executed an advance directive. Not one student raised a hand! That is a serious problem.

Types of Advance Directives

There are several kinds of advance directives.

The Living Will

A living will is the oldest and simplest advance directive. A written statement by you, outlining what you wish for end-of-life care and procedures, it may or may not be legally binding, depending on the state you're in. See Appendix E for a typical living will. It does not require a lawyer to execute and needs only a witness to one's signature. Even in states where it is not binding, the living will remains a very important document and is usually given great weight by those persons (family or physician) who are making decisions for you when you no longer can speak for yourself. We all should have a living will even when more binding and complicated advance directives are implemented. A living will can complement the medical proxy document (see the next section) in that it provides more detailed instructions to the person appointed as proxy and helps guide decisions.

The Medical Proxy Document (Durable Power of Attorney for Health Care Decisions)

The medical proxy is a more powerful, legal form of advance directive that lawyers may term a durable power of attorney for medical affairs. With this document, you delegate to a legally appointed agent (proxy) the power to make health care decisions when you are no longer able to do so. The directive takes effect only when and if you lose the necessary mental competence to participate in medical decision making.

The medical proxy represents a very important advance in the history of end-of-life rights because it gives to a duly appointed agent the right to speak for you in medical decision making in the same way and with the same authority as you would have were you still competent. For this reason, it is vastly more powerful legally than a living will. All states now have some form of medical proxy laws, and *every adult* should execute one now—not waiting until sudden illness or incapacity strikes. A typical medical proxy document is found in Appendix F. As with the living will, it does not require a lawyer, only two witnesses.

There is some debate about how specifically the document should instruct the agent. Some say it is better to give a broad and general delegation of power for the agent to act in ways that are in accordance with your wishes as understood by the agent—not specifying details of what is wanted or not wanted, but rather relying on the fact that you have discussed with your agent the sort of care you desire. We cannot predict all eventualities, and it is better to have the proxy instructed in general terms. In this scenario, the agent decides what is best for you based on his or her knowledge of the sort of care you wish, and there is no detailed written evidence of your wishes.

Others, however, want specificity about wishes in an attachment to the proxy document. Proxy forms have a place in which such further stipulations may be added. I've seen in my years of practice many things I do or do not want for myself and have assembled these into an addendum to my own personal medical proxy document (see Appendix F). This optional addendum of wishes can also be used as a stand-alone memorandum to your agent, quite apart from the proxy document. The latter course is perhaps best: Your agent has the power and knows what you want. If you elect to make this additional statement (attached to the proxy or not), this does not restrict the broad authority the agent has to make decisions in unanticipated situations. Specifying details about any given situation that does not imply the agent should act or not act in a certain way about issues not addressed specifically. You do not have to cover all eventualities in order to empower your agent to act on any problem that might arise.

Medical proxy laws now exist in all fifty states. There is variation in these laws, but the basic principles are the same. A medical proxy document executed in one state will be honored in other states.

Do-Not-Resuscitate Orders

Do-not-resuscitate (DNR) orders are binding documents that instruct emergency personnel (emergency medical technicians, ambulance crews, fire departments, emergency room personnel, and staff personnel of a nursing home or hospital—anyone responding to a call for emergency help) not to undertake resuscitative measures in an attempt to revive you when a sudden collapse has occurred. Such a sudden collapse might be a stroke with loss of consciousness, acute fall in blood pressure, or cessation of heartbeat or breathing. These DNR orders usually require that your condition is terminal with death expected within six months, and there are state health department regulations about what is necessary to put these orders into effect. These requirements may vary according to whether you are in a home situation or in a hospital. They are all time-limited orders that must be renewed within a certain period.

The purpose of these orders is to allow those caring for you to call for emergency help to deal with a new situation or need for transfer to a health care facility for a different type of care—without at the same time risking the aggressive application of resuscitative measures that all medical emergency personnel are bound to undertake when the end-of-life situation is not documented in writing. The DNR is not put in place until you are facing the end of life in the near future, and emergency support and resuscitation are unwanted and inappropriate.

Documentation of DNR orders is done in the medical records at home, nursing homes, and hospitals utilizing special state-approved forms that emergency personnel must see before agreeing not to resuscitate. The form is completed by your physician at your request. A verbal request to emergency personnel for no resuscitation by family or caregiver is not sufficient. A bracelet or necklace indicating the presence of such a DNR order should be used, or the DNR order should be posted at the head of your bed.

It should be remembered that one of the best ways (in addition to DNR orders) to avoid unwanted resuscitative measures for a dying patient at home is not to call for help from 911. These calls automatically trigger emergency teams with their strict rules of engagement, whereas a call to the physician's office instead can initiate comfort measures upon which there is prior agreement. This is another reason for discussing all this with your physician and enlisting his or her cooperation. Almost all calls for end-of-life assistance should be done through the physician's office. This includes the situation in which the family thinks the patient has died. If your own physician is off duty, the call will go most likely to a designated covering physician who may be unfamiliar with the situation, but even so, this person is far easier to convince that no aggressive treatment is indicated than is an emergency ambulance crew. In any event, you will need to rely on written evidence for no aggressive intervention (a copy of the DNR order, living will, and/or proxy document— all of which should be readily at hand).

Advance Directives and Dementia: A Special Dilemma

Alzheimer's disease and certain other dementias, as we saw in Chapter 11, pose a particular problem in that it is very difficult to create ahead of time an advance directive that meets the principal wish that most of us have, namely, that we simply do not wish to live in a state of dementia and would prefer death. How to deal with this issue under present laws is very difficult, but I have made some proposals that could partially begin to meet this dilemma. See Appendix G.

REMINDERS ABOUT ADVANCE DIRECTIVES

- Talk with family, friends, and your physician about your advance directives. Remind them regularly that you have written wishes about end-of-life care.
- Ask to see copies of your advance directives in your physician's medical record, nursing home records, hospital records, home care agencies, and hospice groups. Have copies at home, and give copies to your immediate family members and your attorney.
- Take a copy of your advance directives with you if you enter a hospital.
- Be certain to get acquiescence from your physician that your wishes will be honored. If you cannot get such acquiescence, get another physician.
- Do not procrastinate in executing needed advance directives. Do it now while you are able to do so.

What Can Families Do When the Patient Is Incapable of Medical Decision Making and an Advance Directive Does Not Exist?

There is not a problem if the diagnosis and prognosis are clear and if the family and physician agree upon a course of action. Decisions in these situations are made by the concerned parties. They virtually never go to court.

If there are questions about diagnosis and prognosis or if there is disagreement among caregivers and decision makers as to what should be done, the local probate court may be consulted for a ruling. This is usually relatively easy to do legally, and such decisions are generally handled on a fast track. However, it requires the assistance of an attorney.

Application can also be made to the court for a legal guardianship in situations that involve prolonged care and an unclear future. This court assistance is also easily obtained through probate court and is usually not a prolonged process. The court will delegate decision-making authority to an appropriate family member or friend or, if there is no obvious choice, a disinterested party selected by the court.

Although probate courts generally act with dispatch, sometimes the legal aspects of care for a patient who cannot participate in medical decision making become very complicated and prolonged. The Terri Schiavo case in Florida, which played out so prominently in the courts and the newspapers for some years until her death in 2005, is an example of this. In that case, the husband was the closest of kin with the greatest claim to speak for his wife, who was in a persistent vegetative state. However, the problem arose from the fact that Schiavo's parents' disagreement with the course of action asked for by her husband was so tenacious and stubborn that numerous appeals kept coming up in the courts, and the usual course of events was frustrated. In most instances, properly executed advance directives avoid the sort of fiasco seen in the Schiavo case.

The Essentials for Staying in Control

Most of the time you can stay in control at the turning points of life, but determined action is required. The following are the essentials needed if things are to go the way you want them to.

- Know your rights.
- Make sure your role in medical decision making is a meaningful one (i.e., that you are fully informed and a true participant in the process of deciding what to do). You must understand your own medical situation.
- Outline clearly to your family and caregivers what your wishes are, utilizing written advance directives.
- Define each of the turning points as a formal exercise. Adjust your goals accordingly. Make sure your caregivers sign on to the new principle of assisting you through the dying process, utilizing comfort care measures only.
- Ask for the probability of success for any treatment option. Be guided by reasonable probabilities, and don't require certainty in your decision making. Avoid medical futility.
- Appoint a medical proxy and make sure this person knows your wishes.
- Always keep in mind that you are in charge of what happens to you as long as you remain able to participate in decision making. When you are no longer able to do so, your proxy has the same authority as you would have.
- Don't let the system be in charge. Never allow decisions to be made by default—by inaction on your part.
- Remember that the right to refuse any form of treatment is an almost absolute right. There is no difference ethically or legally between stopping a treatment and never having started it in the first place.
- Plan well ahead. Don't wait until the last minute.
- Be aware that you have options that can prevent the dying process from being more prolonged than you wish.

13

ALLOWING A MERCIFUL DEATH

~⦿~

"Allow the incurably ill to choose a merciful death." So stated Jerry Fensterman in his op-ed article in the the *Boston Globe* as he was coping with terminal kidney cancer in early 2006.[1]

> I was so impressed with Jerry Fensterman's discussion of the waning days of his life that I telephoned him to ask if I could meet with him to talk about his article. He buzzed me into the front door of the large old apartment building in Boston and called down the stairwell from the third floor to come up. Trailing a plastic oxygen line, he was short of breath from the effort of simply coming to the door of his apartment, and it took him ten minutes to settle down again. The disease had spread to his lungs. Doing his best to be a gracious host, he was instantly likeable. A picture of his fourteen-year-old son was on the fireplace mantel. "That is the hardest of it all."
>
> Jerry believed that all persons should have the option of hastening death, but in his article he eloquently described how he initially fought his disease with all his might, recognizing his "addiction to life almost at the cellular level." He had tried to live his life to the fullest as he committed himself "to doing everything within my power to extend life." However, as he watched the quality of his life dropping away—"the rewarding aspects of life have inexorably

shrunk"—he recognized that "perhaps the biggest and most profound change I have undergone is that my addiction to life has been 'cured.' I've kicked the habit! I now know how a feeling, loving, rational person could choose death over life, could choose to relieve his suffering as well as that of his loved ones a few months earlier than would happen naturally." He said that he did not know if he would choose physician-assisted suicide, "yet now, I understand in a manner that I never could have before why an enlightened society should, with thoughtful safeguards, allow the incurably ill to choose a merciful death. . . . If you oppose physician-assisted suicide, first try to walk a mile in the shoes of those to whom you would deny this choice. For as surely as I'm now wearing them, they could one day just as easily be on your feet or those of someone you care deeply about."

Jerry had come to a stage in his disease where he understood how a person with incurable, terminal disease might wish for life to end. Most persons can easily empathize with this.

Attitudes Toward Aid-in-Dying

A Harris poll of 1,010 U.S. adults in April 2005 showed that a 70 percent majority favored a law that would "allow doctors to comply with the wishes of a dying patient in severe distress who asks to have his or her life ended."[2] A 67 percent majority specifically wished that their states had an Oregon-like law to allow physician-assisted suicide for terminally ill patients, and a 64 percent majority felt that a 1997 U.S. Supreme Court ruling was wrong when the Court decided that "individuals do not have a constitutional right to doctor-assisted suicide." A 72 percent majority felt that, if they were unconscious without expectation of regaining consciousness, they would wish to have food and water withdrawn.

The public, therefore, is vastly in favor of a progressive approach to hastening death in intolerable situations. What stands in the way of this becoming reality is the religious right minority, which has a disproportionate influence on what actually happens in the courts and legislatures. Conservative extremists are vociferously determined and outspoken. The moderates of the country do not speak out with the same degree of doggedness.

RESPECTING THE BELIEFS OF OTHERS

Daniel Lee, an ethicist from the Hastings Center, has written perceptively about the question of imposing one's own firmly held beliefs on others.[3] He himself feels that physician-assisted suicide is wrong and that it is up to God alone to end life, but at the same time, he recognizes that others hold different opinions about this matter. He properly does not impose his own thoughts on a suffering patient at the end of life who wishes to hasten death. Lee asks, "Do those of us with deep moral reservations about the morality of physician-assisted suicide have any business using the coercive power of government to try to prevent those who disagree with us from doing what they believe is right? Are there any compelling arguments to justify placing legal roadblocks in the way of terminally ill individuals who wish to end their suffering by ending their lives, provided such decisions are made only after thoughtful, careful deliberation in an environment devoid of social pressure?" He answers his own two questions in the negative.

Lee points out the need for "elaborate and fastidious" safeguards to prevent abuse,[4] and cites the Oregon law as providing this, successfully so. He feels that the Oregon experience has shown that there is no slippery slope that leads to abuse of the law, and the safeguards in the Oregon law deserve credit for this. "When all things are considered, the arguments in favor of continued prohibition of physician-assisted suicide are not particularly compelling. This is not to suggest that those of us with deep moral reservations about physician-assisted suicide should swallow our scruples and spearhead legalization campaigns. But it does suggest that we should not stand in the way of thoughtful individuals such as Timothy Quill and Marcia Angell [strong supporters of patient autonomy at the end of life] who favor legalization."

Where to Go from Here?

Occasional circumstances may lead a terminal patient to conclude that he or she is better off with a hastened death than with prolongation of living. Modern comfort care techniques make this an unusual situation, but it occurs at least a few times in the practicing lifetime of a physician.

As a society, we need to work for the legalization of the right of physicians in every state to assist the patient in hastening death in such cases of intolerable suffering. The Oregon law should be replicated in all states.[5] If a patient in that situation of intolerable suffering elects the option for hastened death, the physician should then be able to provide the ultimate in humane and compassionate help—assistance in ending life. Such relief of suffering is part of the spectrum of medical care, and anything less is a disservice to the patient.

The so-called slippery slope, the opening of the door to abuses, is an exaggerated fear in this country. Although there have been some complaints about abuses in jurisdictions abroad, in which euthanasia and/or physician aid-in-dying is legal, the safeguards that exist in the present Oregon law are well written and have effectively prevented abuses. In 2005, after the first seven years of the Oregon law, patients who elected to use physician aid-in-dying represented only about 0.13 percent of total deaths, and the recent annual statistics are relatively steady (see Appendix B). Clearly, physician aid-in-dying has not been abused in Oregon.

In addition to favoring the legalization of physician-assisted dying, I also favor the legal option of euthanasia as being necessary in some situations. It is a goal toward which we should strive in this country since there are persons with intolerable suffering who cannot physically end their own lives, and the physician needs to be able—under carefully controlled circum-stances—to be overt in actually ending life rather than simply assisting in its ending. The countries in which this is legal have found that the end of life for patients who elect euthanasia can not only be peaceful, but truly a "deliverance."

Appendix A

HISTORICAL BACKGROUND OF THE
END-OF-LIFE MOVEMENT AND CURRENT
NATIONAL ORGANIZATIONS

In this country, the end-of-life movement started in 1938 in the (then) rather radical Euthanasia Society of America. This group was ahead of public opinion on hastening death at the end of life, and it did not score great success. The next several decades brought about a series of successor organizations with evolving missions—changes aiming at capitalizing on what was thought at the moment to be politically possible. In 1974, the Euthanasia Society changed its name to the Society for the Right to Die, reasoning that this would have greater public acceptance, and the Euthanasia Educational Fund (an arm of the Euthanasia Society) similarly evolved into a successor organization, Concern for Dying. For the next fifteen to twenty years the Society for the Right to Die functioned as the political activist group that lobbied for legislation to protect patients' rights, and Concern for Dying functioned as an educational group that eschewed controversial stands; neither organization officially espoused euthanasia.

People continued to speak out for a more active role for the physician in hastening death, a trend that, beginning in the 1970s, was to steadily increase in the last two decades of the century. Among others, Sidney Rosoff, a New York City attorney who was a prominent leader in the right-to-die movement, began to evolve his position along more active lines. He believed that "individuals should have the right to have suffering terminated at their request."[1] Derek Humphry, who assisted his first wife in her dying with cancer in England, vigorously advocated for patients' rights to end life in situations of intolerable distress. In 1991, Humphry published a best seller, *Final Exit*, which described in detail how one might carry out suicide through "self deliverance." It remains a best seller today in subsequent editions.[2]

THE HEMLOCK SOCIETY AND ITS SUCCESSOR, END-OF-LIFE CHOICES

In 1980, Humphry founded the Hemlock Society USA, an organization that vigorously and publicly worked for legalization of physician-assisted suicide—with legalized euthanasia as an eventual goal. During the 1980s, the Hemlock Society was regarded as a fringe group as it promoted its agenda of physician-assisted dying and "self-deliverance" for the intolerably suffering. In the 1990s, however, it developed increasing recognition, influence, and membership, and in 2003 it continued to advocate vigorously under a changed name, End-of-Life Choices. With local chapters throughout the country, it became one of the foremost organizations promoting these goals. In the organization's own words, they were "a nonprofit membership association of people who support choice and dignity at the end of life, or who want authoritative, reliable information to prepare for the final chapters of life. . . . Members have access to information, counselors and programs that help them and their loved ones examine the full range of their end-of-life options, including the option of hastening the dying process." The organization was committed to "maximizing the options for a good death, including the legalization of physician aid in dying for the terminally ill, mentally competent adults who request it under careful safeguards."[3]

End-of-Life Choices (the old Hemlock Society) strongly advocated publicly for these principles and for changes in the law that would facilitate them. It also developed two programs in the last few years that were helpful to individual members. The first, the Caring Friends program, "offer[ed] free, in-home counseling to those with irreversible illnesses who want to explore the full range of their end-of-life options, including the option of hastening their dying. This program [was] operated by healthcare professionals and a team of more than 100 trained volunteers. . . . The participation of a doctor [was] not required, and the program [was] legal in all fifty states." The Caring Friends personnel were careful to stay within the law in that they did not provide physical assistance to the patient who wished to end life, nor did they provide the means for doing so. The second program, the Patient Advocacy program, provided support to members who needed help in having their advance health-care directives followed.

COMPASSION IN DYING

Compassion in Dying, another important activist organization with goals similar to those of the Hemlock Society, was incorporated in Oregon in 1993 with the aim of helping the dying patient. Its Web site stated that

> *Compassion* reaches the public . . . to inform people of the options at the end of life and urge a vigorous societal response to inadequate end-of-life care. We bring all options to the discussion, including high dose pain medication, withdrawing medical treatment, stopping eating and drinking, terminal sedation and aid-in-dying when a patient's suffering continues and treatment is inadequate or unacceptable. . . . We counsel patients and their families in how to access intensive pain management, comfort or hospice care, and . . . talk about safe, effective methods for hastening death.[4]

The organization, a national federation, offered training programs and professional oversight to its staff and volunteers. Similar to End-of-Life Choices, Compassion in Dying did "not disseminate information about aid-in-dying to the public, but shared it in the context of [a] therapeutic relationship with a client." Compassion in Dying's affiliate in Oregon worked with Oregonians to ensure that there was "safe and responsible access to that state's Death with Dignity Act."[5] (See Appendix B.) Most patients who used the Oregon law to end their lives were helped in some way by Compassion in Dying.[6]

Their national federation used the experience gained in Oregon to help other areas of the country through an active legal advocacy program. They helped win a landmark court decision in pain care when they brought to the U.S. Supreme Court questions of Constitutional protection for aid-in-dying. This decision included recognition of undertreated pain as a form of elder abuse. Compassion in Dying also prepared and submitted complaints of inadequate care to medical regulatory boards and the Joint Commission on Accreditation of Healthcare Organizations. They represented patients in the very important court dispute the State of Oregon had with the U.S. Attorney General over his attempt to circumvent the Oregon Death with Dignity Act. The federation was also active legislatively, sponsoring and helping to develop bills dealing with medical education about aid-in-dying, and they had extensive public information programs in which they cooperated with local task forces and coalitions on end-of-life care.[7]

MERGER: THE NEW COMPASSION AND CHOICES

In late 2004, End-of-Life Choices and Compassion in Dying merged under a new name, Compassion and Choices. Proponents of this action, a move that was not supported by all members of the two organizations, felt that the action would result in a stronger and more unified advocacy for the movement. The newly merged Compassion and Choices vowed that its efforts in the future would continue to address both the service-to-members approach and the legislative and legal arenas—these two areas reflecting the strengths of the predecessor organizations. The merger did result in increased efficiencies although the joining together had its difficult moments.

Compassion and Choices provides a broad array of end-of-life support through its client services department for anyone who contacts them. They do not distinguish clients by diagnoses. With regard to persons not in a terminal phase of illness, they will "provide information about hastening death by stopping medical therapies . . . and stopping eating and drinking. These options are the legal right of every mentally capable adult in the United States. For those who are in the terminal phase of their illness and who are mentally capable, other options for hastening death may be discussed, such as the use of medications and helium. [The] definition of terminal is not limited to a six-month life expectancy. Two volunteers and/or staff may be present when a client hastens death, if requested."[8]

FINAL EXIT NETWORK

When the merger above was being contemplated in late 2004, a new group was formed, Final Exit Network, aimed entirely at service to members, not to legislative lobbying or advocacy in the courts. Final Exit Network operates nationally with low-budget, hands-on methods of service to members (only), offering trained "exit guides" who will go to the patient's home to discuss their options for ending intolerable suffering (as does Compassion and Choices). A patient entered into their Exit Guide program does not have to have a terminal illness to receive services of the program. Final Exit Network serves people "suffering from cancer; neurological diseases such as Alzheimer's, Parkinson's, Huntington's, and multiple sclerosis; muscular dystrophy; ALS (Lou Gehrig's disease); respiratory diseases such as emphysema; congestive heart failure; strokes; AIDS; and many . . . others. . . . We do not charge members for these services."[9] Final Exit Network does not actively assist anyone in the act of hastening death, and they carefully comply with all applicable federal and state laws.[10]

Final Exit Network was accepted into membership of the World Federation of Right to Die Societies at the September 2004 meeting in Tokyo, the application having been presented by Derek Humphry. A summary of their goals and methods can be found on their Web site (see Appendix D).

Death with Dignity National Center

In 2003, similar to the merger resulting in Compassion and Choices, Oregon Death with Dignity Legal Defense and Education Center merged with Death with Dignity National Center, and the two are now jointly known as the Death with Dignity National Center.

In their own words:

> The Death with Dignity National Center (DDNC) is the organization that has successfully proposed, passed, defended and helped implement a first-in-the nation law [the Oregon law] that allows terminally ill individuals meeting stringent safeguards, to hasten their own deaths. . . .
>
> DDNC works with leaders in other states considering Oregon-style laws, as legislatures, medical communities and the public come to understand the law's benefits as well as the choice, control and comfort that the law affords.[11]

The group is a very important advocacy organization that has been in the thick of the legal and legislative battles of the last decade, and it had a major role in defending the Oregon law in federal courts. At the same time DDNC allocates just over 50 percent of its budget to public education on end-of-life issues.

Need for One Political and Strategic Approach in This Country

The right-to-die movement in this country has suffered from the problems of advocates not being on the same political footing with regard to the best way to promote their goals. This has been true for a half century. The pathway to the present has been difficult, as evidenced by the new groups formed, the splitting off of factions from established groups, merging of organizations, the split boards of directors, the problems in settling strategic approaches, and the inability to agree on the allocation of financial resources. With the recent merger of the two biggest players into Compassion and Choices, the strategy for the movement will be much clearer. The leaders of all these organizations are trying to move forward cooperatively. The goals are certainly the same.

Euthanasia Research and Guidance Organization (ERGO)

In 1993, Derek Humphry, founder of the Hemlock Society, formed the Euthanasia Research and Guidance Organization (ERGO) to share information about the end-of-life movement. In Humphry's words, "ERGO has enormous contacts with scholars, students, and media, and we've sold thousands of books about aspects of euthanasia all over the world, and in many languages."[12] The organization has utilized the Internet heavily in its communications, and Humphry regards it as a grassroots effort on a large scale. Their combined Web sites have over 1,000 hits per day, and on its news listserv they communicate with over 1,200 persons daily. ERGO has provided important financial backing to NuTech, a research group that investigates new methods of self-deliverance. Humphry describes ERGO as having "no offices, just an incorporated board, but it's my guess we are in touch with more people than the other groups." Its

Internet and mailing addresses are in Appendix D, and general contact information for all the organizations discussed in this appendix can also be found there.

Dr. Jack Kevorkian, Historically a Special Case

Dr. Jack Kevorkian's public actions started with assisted suicide and then led into the clearly illegal territory of euthanasia. In effect, he dared the system to put him in jail, and it eventually did. Regardless of what one thinks of his style (it was upsetting to many physicians and others), he brought the questions of physician-assisted suicide and euthanasia to the public's attention in a way that no other person previously had been able to do. He was willing to go to prison for his strong belief that intolerably suffering patients have the right to end life, or to have it ended for them at their request. He remains in prison at the time this book was written, apparently in very poor health.

I admire his courage and tenacity.

Hospice Movement

Any discussion of the evolution of end-of-life care in the last fifty years must recognize the extremely important role the hospice movement has had in improving care of the dying. The hospice movement worldwide, the national effort in this country, and the local hospice organizations in our hometowns have all been critical in this improvement. Hospice care is now a fully matured program that gives psychological, spiritual, and hands-on care of the terminally ill, and their practices of pain control and other important aspects of comfort care have set standards for us all to emulate. They work in conjunction with the patient's physicians and other caregivers in the system—not supplanting other parts of the system but working together with them.

Hospice is integral to any history of end-of-life care, but not because hospice advocates hastening death. Quite the contrary, hospice firmly states its position as neither hastening nor preventing death. They feel strongly that if comfort care is given properly, there should be no reason for a patient to wish to end his or her life. For the most part, I agree with this, except that I do feel that there are very occasional instances in which everything is done right, yet the patient continues to suffer intolerably. In that circumstance, hastening the end is an option the patient should have.

Hospice services have not been reimbursed by insurance unless they are performed in the terminal phase, which has usually been defined as the last six months of a fatal illness. Hospice workers have often pointed out that they are much more effective in helping the patient when they are called in early in the terminal illness rather than late. What has happened often is that the physician or other referring person waits until too late in the illness, and hospice then has to scramble in order to build a trusting relationship and to put into practice their concepts of comfort care for the terminally ill. All parties—patient, family, physician, and other caregivers—have benefited when hospice enters the picture at an appropriately early time so they can work most effectively and with the greatest result.

Appendix B
Oregon and Physician-assisted Dying

~~◦∾~~

Oregon's Legal Experiment with Assisted Dying

In 1994, Oregon Death with Dignity was founded for the purpose of promoting the legal right for patients with terminal illness to receive overt physician assistance in ending life. The efforts of this group were successful, and in that same year, the citizens of the state approved the Death with Dignity Act in a referendum. The Act allowed physicians legally to prescribe a medication that could be taken voluntarily by an informed patient to end life in certain terminal situations and under certain circumstances, described in the next section.

The Death with Dignity Act initially met with various attempts to nullify it legally, and its implementation did not occur until 1997. Subsequently, in 2001, U.S. Attorney General John Ashcroft attempted to prevent physicians from continuing to write prescriptions in conjunction with the Oregon law, but he and his successor were rebuffed by the courts. The matter reached the U. S. Supreme Court, which ruled in January 2006 that the Attorney General had overstepped his authority. It was a narrowly drawn opinion that did not address constitutional issues, but it nevertheless allowed the Oregon law to remain operative.

The Oregon Law's Provisions

The Oregon law states that it is legal for a doctor to prescribe a barbiturate for the purpose of the patient ending life when he or she is expected to die within six months from a terminal illness and when other stipulations are met.

- The patient must be an adult who is eighteen years of age or older, has lived in Oregon for at least six months, and makes a voluntary, written request to the physician for such assistance, plus two additional oral requests separated by at least fifteen days and documented in the record by the physician.
- The request must be witnessed by two persons who attest that the request is voluntary and not a result of coercion.
- Two independent physicians must attest that the disease is terminal with less than six months until death is expected.
- The patient must be fully informed as to the diagnosis and prognosis, and the physician must attest that the patient is capable of making medical decisions.
- The consequences of taking the medication must be fully understood, namely, that it will produce death. Feasible alternatives such as comfort care, hospice care, and pain control must be understood by the patient.
- The patient must be able to self-administer the medication.
- The physician must document in the medical record the diagnosis, prognosis, potential risks of taking the medication, the result of taking the medication, and the feasible alternatives, including, but not limited to, hospice care, symptom control, and comfort care. The physician must attest that he or she has informed the patient of the right to rescind the request.
- The prescribing physician must obtain a consultation with a second doctor who confirms the diagnosis and prognosis and attests that the patient is capable, acting voluntarily, and making an informed decision. Counseling with a psychiatrist or psychologist must be requested if either the prescribing physician or the consulting physician questions the patient's capability to make an informed choice or judgment.
- The prescribing physician must request that the patient notify the next of kin of the prescription request.
- The patient must be offered opportunity to rescind the request.
- The patient must be an Oregon resident.
- There must be no denial of insurance as a result of the action.
- The physician must report to the Oregon Public Health Services what has happened along with documentation that all

requirements have been met, as stated previously. The names
of the doctor and the patient are kept confidential.

These requirements have been exceedingly well thought out, and
they provide strong and reliable protection against the possibility of
abuse.

USE OF THE OREGON LAW

Since the Oregon law became operative in 1997, 246 persons have
died in the first eight years through the end of 2005, utilizing lethal
prescriptions for barbiturates in accordance with the provisions of the
law. This is not a large number of people who have taken their lives
in this way. The number of such deaths annually increased only
slowly for the first five years the law was in effect, and since 2002, the
number has remained relatively stable (39 in 2005). These numbers
are small (approximately 0.13 percent) relative to the overall number
of deaths in Oregon—approximately 30,000 annually.

The numbers are striking in several ways. First, the number of times
prescriptions have been written and utilized relative to the number of
deaths in the state during that time is very small, indicating that there
has been no rush to utilize the option. Second, the number of people
who actually took the medication, compared to the number of patients who obtained a prescription for it (60 prescriptions and 37
deaths in 2004, for example) indicates that the mere possession of the
means to end intolerable suffering is sufficiently reassuring to many
patients that the necessity of taking their life is obviated. Third, there
has not been a single known case of abuse of the spirit or letter of the
law. Lastly, the rate of complications (failure to achieve a rapid and
peaceful death) has been extremely low (see the report that follows).
The data speaks for itself to the opponents of the law, indicating no
evidence for a "slippery slope" once the door was opened.

As indicated in the latest annual report (that follows), the reasons
people have cited for taking their lives under the provisions of this
law have been (in order of decreasing importance): loss of autonomy—86 percent; less able to engage in activities that make life enjoyable—85 percent; losing control of bodily functions—57 percent;
burden on family, friends, and caregivers—37 percent; inadequate

pain control—22 percent; and financial implication of treatment—3 percent.

See the excerpts from the Eighth Annual Report on Oregon's Death With Dignity Act (that follows) for more details of how this law has operated so successfully.

Eighth Annual Report on Oregon's Death with Dignity Act

The following sections have been excerpted from the Eighth Annual Report on Oregon's Death with Dignity Act, which was released by the Department of Human Services, Oregon State Public Health, on March 9, 2006. The full twenty-four-page report can be found on the Web at www.oregon.gov/DHS/ph/pas/docs/year8.pdf.

Contributing Editor: Richard Leman, MD
Data Analysis: David Hopkins, MS
State Epidemiologist: Metvin A. Kohn, MD, MPH
This assessment was conducted as part of the required surveillance and public health practice activities of the Department of Human Services and was supported by Department funds. For more information, contact: Darcy Niemeyer, Department of Human Services, Oregon State Public Health, Office of Disease Prevention and Epidemiology, 800 N.E. Oregon Street, Suite 730, Portland, OR 97232, e-mail: darcy.niemeyer@state.or.us, 971-673-0982, Fax: 971-673-0994, www.oregon.gov/DHS/ph/pas/index.shtml.

Summary

Physician-assisted suicide (PAS) has been legal in Oregon since November 1997, when Oregon voters approved the Death with Dignity Act (DWDA) for the second time (see History). The Department of Human Services (DHS) is legally required to collect information regarding compliance with the Act and make the information available on a yearly basis. In this eighth annual report, we characterize 38 Oregonians who died in 2005 following ingestion of medications prescribed under provisions of the Act, and look at whether the numbers and characteristics of these patients differ from those who used PAS in prior years. Patients choosing PAS were identified through mandated physician and pharmacy reporting. Our information comes from these reports, physician interviews and death certificates. We also compare the demographic characteristics of patients participating during 1998–2005 with other Oregonians who died of the same underlying causes.

In 2005, 39 physicians wrote a total of 64 prescriptions for lethal doses of medication. In 1998, 24 prescriptions were written, followed by 33 in 1999, 39 in 2000, 44 in 2001, 58 in 2002, 68 in 2003, and 60 in 2004. Thirty-two of the 2005 prescription recipients died after ingesting the medication. Of the 32 recipients who did not ingest the prescribed medication in 2005, 15 died from their illnesses, and 17 were alive on December 31, 2005. In addition, six patients who received prescriptions during 2004 died in 2005 as a result of ingesting the prescribed medication, giving a total of 38 PAS deaths during 2005. One 2004 prescription recipient, who ingested the prescribed medication in 2005, became unconscious 25 minutes after ingestion, then regained consciousness 65 hours later. This person did not obtain a subsequent prescription and died 14 days later of the underlying illness (17 days after ingesting the medication).

After an initial increase in PAS use during the first five years the Act was in effect, the number of Oregonians who use PAS remained relatively stable since 2002. In 1998, 16 Oregonians used PAS, followed by 27 in 1999, 27 in 2000, 21 in 2001, 38 in 2002, 42 in 2003, and 37 in 2004. The ratio of PAS deaths to total deaths trended upward during 1998–2003, peaking at 13.6 [per 10,000] in 2003 and has since remained stable. In 1998 there were 5.5 PAS deaths per every 10,000 total deaths, followed by 9.2 in 1999, 9.1 in 2000, 7.1 in 2001, 12.2 in 2002, 13.6 in 2003, 12.3 in 2004, and an estimated 12/10,000 in 2005.

Compared to all Oregon decedents in 2005, PAS participants were more likely to have malignant neoplasms (84% vs. 24%), to be younger (median age 70 vs. 78 years), and to have more formal education (37% vs. 15% had at least a baccalaureate degree).

During the past eight years, the 246 patients who took lethal medications differed in several ways from the 74,967 Oregonians dying from the same underlying diseases. Rates of participation in PAS decreased with age, although over 65% of PAS users were age 65 or older. Rates of participation were higher among those who were divorced or never married, those with more years of formal education, and those with amyotrophic lateral sclerosis, HIV/AIDS, or malignant neoplasms (see Patient Characteristics).

Physicians indicated that patient requests for lethal medications stemmed from multiple concerns, with eight in 10 patients having at least three concerns. The most frequently mentioned end-of-life concerns during 2005 were: a decreasing ability to participate in activities that made life enjoyable, loss of dignity, and loss of autonomy (see End-of-Life Concerns).

Complications were reported for three patients during 2005; two involved regurgitation, and, as noted above, one patient regained consciousness after ingesting the prescribed medication. None involved seizures (see Complications). Fifty percent of patients became unconscious within five minutes of ingestion of the lethal medication and the same percentage died within 26 minutes of ingestion. The range of time from ingestion to death was from five minutes to 9.5 hours. Emergency Medical Services were called for one patient in order to pronounce death.

The number of terminally ill patients using PAS has remained small, with about 1 in 800 deaths among Oregonians in 2005 resulting from physician-assisted suicide.

Lethal Medication

During 1998–2004, secobarbital was the lethal medication prescribed for 101 of the 208 patients (49%). During 2005, as during previous years, all lethal medications prescribed under the provisions of the DWDA were barbiturates. In 2005, 34 patients (89%) used pentobarbital and 4 patients (11%) used secobarbital. Since the DWDA was implemented, 56% of the PAS patients used pentobarbital, 43% used secobarbital, and 2% used other medications. (Three used secobarbital/amobarbital, and one used secobarbital and morphine).

End-of-Life Concerns

Providers were asked if, based on discussions with patients, any of seven end-of-life concerns might have contributed to the patients' requests for lethal medication. In nearly all cases, physicians reported multiple concerns contributing to the request. The most frequently reported concerns included a decreasing ability to participate in activities that make life enjoyable (89%), loss of dignity (89%), and losing autonomy (79%).

Comments

Since 2002, both the number of prescriptions written for physician-assisted suicide and the number of terminally ill patients taking lethal medication have remained relatively stable with about 1 in 800 deaths among Oregonians in 2005 resulting from physician-assisted suicide. A large population study of dying Oregonians published in 2004 found that 17% considered PAS seriously enough to have discussed the matter with their family and that about 2% of patients formally requested PAS. Of the 1,384 decedents for whom information was gathered, one had received a prescription for lethal medication and did not take it. No unreported cases of PAS were identified.

Overall, smaller numbers of patients appear to use PAS in Oregon compared to the Netherlands. However, as detailed in previous reports, our numbers are based on a reporting system for terminally ill patients who legally receive prescriptions for lethal medications, and do not include patients and physicians who may act outside the provisions of the DWDA.

Over the last eight years, the rate of PAS among patients with ALS in Oregon has been substantially higher than among patients with other illnesses. This finding is consistent with other studies. In the Netherlands, where both PAS and euthanasia are openly practiced, one in five ALS patients died as a result of PAS or euthanasia. A study of Oregon and Washington ALS patients found that one-third of these patients discussed wanting PAS in the last month of life. Though numbers are small, and results must be interpreted with caution, Oregon HIV/AIDS patients are also more likely to use PAS.

Physicians have consistently reported that concerns about loss of autonomy, loss of dignity, and decreased ability to participate in activities that make life enjoyable are important motivating factors in patient requests for lethal medication across all eight years. Interviews with family members during 1999 corroborated physician reports.

These findings were supported by a study of hospice nurses and social workers caring for PAS patients in Oregon.

While it may be common for patients with a terminal illness to consider PAS, a request for PAS can be an opportunity for a medical provider to explore with patients their fears and wishes around end-of-life care, and to make patients aware of other options. Often once the provider has addressed a patient's concerns, he or she may choose not to pursue PAS.

Appendix C
The International Scene

ᕙᕗ

The Netherlands, Belgium, and Switzerland: Legalized Assisted Dying

In The Netherlands in the early 1980s, the national medical society outlined the circumstances under which it felt doctors might ethically end the lives of suffering, terminally ill patients by euthanasia, but there was no law that allowed euthanasia. It was simply the doctors saying that such action was ethical and in the best interests of their patients. The prosecutors and the legal system looked the other way, and euthanasia was practiced (reasonably) openly.

However, in 2002, the Parliament of The Netherlands finally wrote into law permission for doctors to perform euthanasia, adopting the requirements the medical society had previously laid out. The patient must be completely informed and must be competent to make such a request. The euthanasia must be voluntary and in response to more than one request, and there are other limiting conditions that protect against abuse, similar to the Oregon law. As of 2005, about 3,800 Dutch a year opt for a fatal injection from a physician or a prescribed overdose.[1]

Belgium, acting similarly in 2002, also passed a euthanasia law for people of sound mind but "futile medical condition." In early 2005, deaths by euthanasia were occurring at a rate of about thirty per month, about 60 percent of which occurred in the hospital and the rest at home.[2]

In Switzerland, it has been legal since 1941 for physicians to assist in suicide but not carry out euthanasia. "More than 2,000 people have received medically prescribed doses of barbiturates to kill themselves in Switzerland over the past 10 years, according to figures kept by the three main suicide organizations. So-called assisted suicide is legal here as long as the agencies that arrange death do so for 'honorable reasons,' without seeking profit, although they may charge basic fees. Dignitas [a private group in Zurich that will assist patients in suicide] has raised concerns among prosecutors in other European countries by facilitating the suicides of non-Swiss, a legal gray area, arranging everything from travel tickets to funeral services, as well as the fatal dose."[3] Dignitas has helped 493 individuals end their lives since 1998.

EXIT Deutsche Schweiz is another similar organization operating in Switzerland. During the 1990s EXIT Deutsche Schweiz "offered instruction and personal guidance through suicide to members who suffer from diseases with 'poor prognosis, unbearable suffering or un-reasonable disability' and wish to die. It currently has more than 50,000 members, almost 1% of Switzerland's population. The propor-tion of the total number of Swiss patients suffering multiple sclerosis, amyotrophic lateral sclerosis or HIV/AIDS who chose to end their lives with assistance from Exit (4.5%, 3.4%, and 1.7% respectively) was markedly higher than in cancer patients (0.5%)."[4] Details of these 748 cases have been reviewed.[5]

These countries (along with Oregon) are the only jurisdictions at present in which these actions are legal.

AUSTRALIA: A SPECIAL CASE

Australia has been particularly active in the arena of hastening death under prescribed circumstances. In 1995, the Northern Territory Par-liament passed an act allowing euthanasia and assisted suicide, and four people utilized that law to hasten death, all with guidance from euthanasia advocate Dr. Philip Nitschke. In 1997, the national par-liament overturned the Northern Territory law, but Dr. Nitschke has continued his activism.[6]

DYING WITH DIGNITY, CANADA

Dying with Dignity is Canada's active "voice for choice at the end of life."[7] This organization has goals similar to those of groups in the United States: "Our mission as a national non-profit organization is to improve quality of dying and to expand end-of-life choices in

Canada . . . by educating, by informing, and by providing a confidential support program for individuals faced with making important end-of-life decisions." It also advocates for legislative change that includes physician aid-in-dying, if a patient so chooses.

WORLD FEDERATION OF RIGHT-TO-DIE SOCIETIES

In 1980 at a conference in Oxford, England, the World Federation of Right-to-Die Societies was organized, indicating the extent to which the movement has spread to many countries. Derek Humphry and Sidney Rosoff were among the organizers. The Federation began with twenty-seven societies from eighteen countries and subsequently has grown to thirty-eight societies in twenty-three countries. It holds biennial conferences at various places around the world to discuss right-to-die issues, and representatives of the Federation have made many presentations to medical ethics groups, geriatric organizations, and human rights conferences. It publishes regular newsletters and disseminates information about the movement.[8]

Appendix D
END-OF-LIFE ORGANIZATIONS

Compassion and Choices
P.O. Box 101810
Denver, CO 80250-1810
Phone: 800-247-7421
Web site: www.compassionandchoices.org
E-mail: info@compassionindying.org

Death with Dignity National Center
520 SW 6th Avenue, Suite 1030
Portland, OR 97204
Phone: 503-228-4415
Web site: www.deathwithdignity.org
E-mail: info@deathwithdignity.org

Death with Dignity Vermont, Inc.
708 Wake Robin Drive
Shelburne, VT 05482
Phone: 802-985-9473
Web site: www.deathwithdignityvermont.org
E-mail: info@deathwithdignityvermont.org

Dignitas
Zurich, Switzerland
Web site: www.dignitas.ch
E-mail: dignitas@dignitas.ch

Dying with Dignity, Canada
55 Eglinton Avenue East, Suite 802
Toronto, Ontario M4P 1G8
Phone: 800-495-6156
Web site: www.dyingwithdignity.ca
E-mail: info@dyingwithdignity.ca

Eighth Annual Report on Oregon's Death With Dignity Act
Oregon Department of Human Services
Office of Disease Prevention and Epidemiology
800 NE Oregon Street
Portland, OR 97232
Phone: 800-422-6012

Euthanasia Research and Guidance Organization (ERGO)
24829 Norris Lane
Junction City, OR 97448-9552
Phone: 541-998-1873
Web site: www.finalexit.org
E-mail: ergo@efn.org

Final Exit Network
P.O. Box 965005
Marietta, GA 30066
Phone: 800-524-3948
Web site: www.finalexitnetwork.org
E-mail: info@finalexitnetwork.org

World Federation of Right to Die Societies
Web site: www.worldrtd.net

Appendix E
SAMPLE LIVING WILL

A living will simply states your wishes for end-of-life care. It is not legally binding, but usually it is honored. It can be an extremely useful instrument in conjunction with a medical proxy statement (which is a legal assignment of decision-making power to an agent that becomes operative when and if you are no longer able to speak for yourself). The living will can be appended to your medical proxy statement as an optional addendum. It may say anything you wish regarding your preferences, and the following is a sample only. Alter it in any way you wish. It does not require an attorney—only a witness, preferably two.

Living Will Declaration

To my family, doctors, and all those concerned with my care:

I, _____, being of sound mind, make this statement as a directive to be followed if for any reason I become unable to participate in decisions regarding my medical care.

I direct that life-sustaining procedures should be withheld or withdrawn if I have an illness, disease, or injury, or experience extreme mental deterioration, such that there is no reasonable expectation of recovering or regaining a meaningful quality of life. Life-sustaining procedures that may be withheld or withdrawn include, but are not limited to: surgery, antibiotics, cardiopulmonary resuscitation, respiratory support, and artificially administered feeding and fluids.

I further direct that treatment be limited to comfort measures only. I wish medication for pain and other distress to be used liberally in doses sufficient to relieve my symptoms, even if such medication were to shorten my life.

Other Personal Instructions

These directions express my legal right to refuse treatment. Therefore, I expect my family, doctors, and all those concerned with my care to regard themselves as morally bound to act in accord with my wishes, and, in so doing, to be free from any liability for having followed my directions.

Signed: _____ Date: _____

Witness: _____

Witness: _____

Appendix F

HEALTH CARE PROXY FORM WITH OPTIONAL ATTACHMENT

⟨⟨⟨⟩⟩⟩

Your birth date: ____/____/____

I, _____, residing at
   Principal: Print your name

_____
Street   *City/Town*   *State/ZIP*

appoint as my health-care agent:

_____ of
Name of person you choose as agent

_____.
Street   *City/Town*   *State/ZIP*   *Telephone*

Optional: If my agent is unwilling/unable to serve, then I appoint as my alternate agent:

_____ of
Name of person you choose as alternate agent

_____.
Street   *City/Town*   *State/ZIP*   *Telephone*

My agent shall have the authority to make all health-care decisions for me, including decisions about life-sustaining treatment, subject to any limitations I state below, if I am unable to make health-care decisions myself. My agent's authority becomes effective if my attending physician determines in writing that I lack the capacity to make or to communicate health-care decisions. My agent is then to have the same authority to make health-care decisions as I would if I had the capacity to make them, EXCEPT (list here the limitations, if any, you wish to place on your agent's authority; if none, enter "none"):

I direct my agent to make health-care decisions based on my agent's assessment of my personal wishes. If my personal wishes are unknown, my agent is to make health-care decisions based on my agent's assessment of my best interests. Photocopies of this Health Care Proxy shall have the same force and effect as the original and may be given to other health-care providers.

An optional statement is attached (check one): ___ yes ___ no
[You may attach to this document, as a guide to your agent, a statement of particular wishes you want followed by your agent. This is not required, and, in its absence, your agent will use his/her discretion to do what he/she feels you would want done, as a result of discussions you have had with your agent.]

Signed:_____

Complete only if principal is unable to sign: I have signed the principal's name above at his/her direction in the presence of the principal and two witnesses.

_____
Name

_____
Street   *City/Town*   *State/ZIP*

Witness statement: We, the undersigned, each witnessed the signing of this Health Care Proxy by the principal or at the direction of the principal and state that the principal appears to be at least eighteen years of age, of sound mind, and under no constraint or undue influence. Neither of us is named as the health-care agent or alternate agent in this document. In our presence this _____ day of _____, _____.
                            Month   *Year*

Witness #1 _____
                  Signature

_____
Print Name   *Address*

Witness #2 _____
                  Signature

_____
Print Name   *Address*

Statements of Health-Care Agent and Alternate Agent
(OPTIONAL)

Health-Care Agent: I have been named by the principal as the principal's health-care agent by this Health Care Proxy. I have read this document carefully, and have personally discussed with the principal his/her health-care wishes at a time of possible incapacity. I know the principal and accept this appointment freely. I am not an operator, administrator or employee of a hospital, clinic, nursing home, rest home, soldiers' home, or other health facility where the principal is presently a patient or resident or has applied for admission. Or, if I am a person so described, I am also related to the principal by blood, marriage, or adoption. If called upon and to the best of my ability, I will try to carry out the principal's wishes.

Signature of Health-Care Agent: _____

Alternate Agent: I have been named by the principal as the principal's alternate agent by this Health Care Proxy. I have read this document carefully, and I have personally discussed with the principal his/her health-care wishes at a time of possible incapacity. I know the principal and accept this appointment freely. I am not an operator, administrator or employee of a hospital, clinic, nursing home, rest home, soldiers' home, or other health facility where the principal is presently a patient or resident or has applied for admission. Or if I am a person so described, I am also related to the principal by blood, marriage, or adoption. If called upon and to the best of my ability, I will try to carry out the principal's wishes.

Signature of Alternate Agent: _____

Optional Attachment to Health Care Proxy Form

[You may attach to your medical proxy statement of optional instructions to your agent—or a page of similar instructions of your own
choosing. I have attached the following to my own medical proxy
document, representing specific things I do or do not wish. You could
use all of it, part of it, or none of it.—SW]

Statement of my particular wishes: I do not want my life to be prolonged nor do I want life-sustaining treatment to be provided or continued if my agent believes the burdens of the treatment outweigh the
expected benefits. My particular wishes are that if I have such an illness, injury or condition, or if I am so mentally impaired that there is
no significant quality of life to my existence, and if there is no reasonable expectation of recovery to a state of good quality of life, or if I
am permanently unconscious (in a "persistent vegetative state"), that
nothing be done to prolong my life, including resuscitative measures
(in the event of hypotension, stopping breathing, or cardiac arrest), the
administration of intravenous and/or nasogastric fluids and nutrition,
the use of respirators or other mechanical devices to sustain life, and
the use of antibiotics for pneumonia or other infection (this list is not
all-inclusive). With respect to nutrition and hydration provided by
means of a nasogastric tube or tube in the stomach, intestines, or
veins, I wish to make clear that I intend to include these procedures
among the "life-sustaining procedures" that may be withheld or withdrawn under the conditions above.

If I am in the circumstances described above and am in a dying
state, I would prefer treatment at home or in a nursing home, with
comfort care being the only objective, as opposed to transfer to a hospital, unless the latter were needed for the accomplishment of comfort
care, and I request that adequate medication be given to control pain
and/or agitation, even if such medication were to result in depressing

respiration or hastening the end of life. I want my agent to consider
the relief of suffering, the expense involved, and the quality as well as
the extension of my life in making the decision concerning life-
sustaining treatment.

Signature of Principal: _____
Date:_____

Signature of Witness #1 _____
Date:_____

Signature of Witness #2 _____
Date:_____

[The statement above, "my particular wishes," can also be used as a
stand-alone memorandum to your health-care agent, instead of being
appended to the agent-appointment document. Many prefer the stand-
alone approach for specifying their particular wishes. In that case, a
statement, such as the one above, functions as living will instructions,
directed to your agent, who has the power to make the necessary decisions on your behalf.]

Appendix G

Proposed Authorization for Ending Life in Situations of Irreversible and Progressive Cognitive Decline

❧❧❧

If you wish to construct a special advance directive for shortening life when and if dementia supervenes in the future, you might consider something along the line of what I have done for myself. This is what I think *should* be available to us all, but is not at present—enabling legislation would be necessary for this to be. The statement is a combination of instructions that are now possible legally and ethically, combined with certain other instructions that I know to be legally problematic (and perhaps impossible). These instructions will be asking more of my appointed agent than she can deliver, but they indicate how strong my *wishes* are about not living in a state of dementia, which strengthens the hand of my agent in trying to do the best she can to honor my requests.

These requests that I have outlined can be attached to one's presently accepted advance directives (proxy designation document and/or standard living will) as supplementary instructions. They can contribute to shortening the duration of dementia in that they indicate that the main thrust of decision making is, *at every turn*, to be toward those actions (or nonactions) that will prevent prolongation of life when dementia has supervened.

You could utilize the following proposals and statements in such a document, constructing a statement for yourself. The following is the sort of thing you might say.[1]

There should be an initial statement concerning your mental competence at the time of signing and your intact ability to make medical

---

184

decisions, which is attested to by a physician. The document would then recognize that you, as a presently competent person, are making a decision that is to be binding on your agent as nearly as possible when and if, at some future time, you suffer from irreversible dementia. The directive would further recognize that you prefer dying to living in a state of dementia.

When this special advance directive is triggered by the onset of dementia (at a stage in the disease discussed next), the first required action of caregivers would be that they not employ any of the treatments or supportive actions outlined below, which would be withheld as unwanted treatment. (Much of this list is like an ordinary living will, but not all.)

- I want no measures taken to prolong my life.
- I wish to be kept comfortable, free of pain, and maintained in a dignified state.
- I wish any medication that is used to keep me comfortable and free of pain or other distress to be in sufficient dosage that distress, physical or psychological, is relieved, even if such medication hastens my death.
- If I get an infection, do not treat it—just make me comfortable. Use no antibiotics.
- If I cannot feed myself, just leave the food for me. Do not spoon feed me or encourage me in any way to eat or drink. Do not treat dehydration with anything other than fluids offered orally, and do not try to encourage drinking beyond what I clearly desire.
- Give me no artificial feeding or hydration of any sort. I do not want a tube inserted to administer food or hydration (no intravenous fluids).
- If I cannot breathe for myself, I do not wish to be put on a ventilator. Oxygen is not to be administered other than possibly for the relief of air hunger. Low oxygen levels in the blood are not a sufficient indication for the use of oxygen.
- If my kidneys fail, I do not want dialysis.
- If I stop breathing or my heart stops beating, I do not want cardiopulmonary resuscitation.

- I want no blood transfusions.
- If I have a heart attack or stroke, do nothing to extend my life, but do provide comfort measures.
- I want no surgery unless it is absolutely necessary to control pain.
- I want no x-rays, blood tests, other laboratory tests, or invasive diagnostic procedures.
- I do not want regular vital signs to be taken, including blood pressure and temperature measurements.
- I do not want to be treated in a hospital, but wish to be made comfortable where I reside.
- Other:_____.

These statements might be followed by a set of criteria defining the sort of dementia with which you would be unwilling to live and would wish further *active* measures to be undertaken to shorten life and the period of suffering, such as the withholding of fluid, accompanied by sedation (terminal dehydration with sedation), which would be the next step beyond withholding unwanted treatment. Such a step would be aimed at hastening death. These criteria (which trigger active measures to shorten life) you could list in detail, indicating which single criterion or which combination of criteria should trigger the withholding of fluids. The criteria I have listed for myself include the following, which you could add to or subtract from.

CRITERIA WITH WHICH I WOULD NOT WANT TO CONTINUE LIVING

- An irreversible condition that causes severe decline in cognitive abilities.
- Inability to recognize family and those loved by me.
- Inability to perform ordinary functions of self care and cleanliness.
- Inability to feed myself.
- Repeated violent or disruptive behavior.
- Disorientation or wandering off frequently.
- Chronic confusion about my situation.
- Incoherence and/or inability to communicate intelligibly.

- Chronic fearfulness or frustration due to cognitive disorder.
- Other:_____.

Under present laws, there is no legal assurance that the criteria above could be used in an advance directive to ensure that caregivers would withhold fluids and administer sedation, but there is an advantage to *requesting* this. Namely, it makes completely clear that the patient absolutely does not wish to live in a state of dementia. It could sway caregivers' opinions as to what should or should not be done in various settings. That probably is the most that can be hoped for with our present laws. In the future, I hope that laws will be passed that will allow this request to be binding if a patient becomes demented.

In my own document, I have stipulated that my wishes have been carefully discussed with my agent and that she understands my wishes. I have stated further that if any of the actions discussed previously causes me to die sooner rather than later, that is my wish since I do not want to live in a state of senile dementia or cognitive impairment that precludes a rewarding and satisfying intellectual life.

A section for signature of the principal, witnesses, and designated agent(s) would follow. There would be no requirement for a notary or an attorney.

A proposal such as the one described in this appendix would reduce the indignity and suffering imposed on persons with dementia, and I feel that such a proposal should ideally become allowed by law in all the states in the near future.

Notes

Preface

1. S. H. Wanzer, et al., "The Physician's Responsibility Toward Hopelessly Ill Patients: A Second Look, *New England Journal of Medicine*
   320 (1989): 844–49.

Chapter 1   Turning Points at Life's End

1. S. H. Wanzer, et al., "The Physician's Responsibility Toward Hopelessly Ill Patients: A Second Look, *New England Journal of Medicine*
   320 (1989): 844–49.
2. T. E. Quill, "Death and Dignity: A Case of Individualized Decision
   Making," *New England Journal of Medicine* 324 (1991): 691–94. Also,
   T. E. Quill, "Dying and Decision Making—Evolution of End-of-Life
   Options," *New England Journal of Medicine* 350 (2004): 2029–32.

Chapter 3   The First Turning Point

1. Last Acts, a national coalition of health-care providers and con-
   sumers dedicated to improving care near the end of life, sponsored a
   task force that prepared a November 2002 report, *Means to a Better
   End: A Report on Dying in America Today* (Last Acts National Program
   Office, 1620 Eye Street NW, Suite 202, Washington, DC
   20006–4017, www.lastacts.org). This ninety-five-page comprehensive
   look at how we deliver comfort care in this country outlined five
   principles of proper palliative care, stating that palliative care:
   - respects the goals, likes, and choices of the dying person;
   - looks after the medical emotional, social, and spiritual needs of
     the dying person;

- supports the needs of the family members;
- helps gain access to needed health-care providers and appropriate care settings; and
- builds ways to provide excellent care at the end of life.

They used the term *palliative care*, but for our purposes the same can be said of comfort care as we define it here.

2. R. S. Morrison and D. E. Meier, "Palliative Care," *New England Journal of Medicine* 350 (2004): 2582–90.

3. S. H. Wanzer, et al. "The Physician's Responsibility Toward Hopelessly Ill Patients: A Second Look," *New England Journal of Medicine* 320 (1989): 844–49.

4. J. M. Teno, B. R. Clarridge, et al., "Family Perspectives on End-of-Life Care at the Last Place of Care," *Journal of the American Medical Association* 291 (2004): 88–93. Study from: Center for Gerontology and Health Care Research, Brown Medical School and Department of Community Health, Brown University, Providence, RI; and the Center for Survey Research, University of Massachusetts at Boston. Family members or other knowledgeable informants representing 1,578 decedents were surveyed by telephone.

CHAPTER 4   PAIN CONTROL

1. R. G. Twycross, "Morphine and Diamorphine in the Terminally Ill Patient," *Acta anaesthesiologica Scandinavica*. Supplementum 74 (1982): 128–34.

2. M. N. Levine, D. L. Sackett, and H. Bush, "Heroin Versus Morphine for Cancer Pain?" *Archives of Internal Medicine* 146 (1986): 353–56.

CHAPTER 5   WHAT YOU SHOULD EXPECT FROM YOUR DOCTORS AND NURSES

1. A. Gawande, *Complications: A Surgeon's Notes on an Imperfect Science* (New York: Metropolitan Books, 2002).

CHAPTER 7   THE SECOND TURNING POINT

1. Timothy Quill, MD, has been a pioneer in raising doctors' awareness of this; see T. E. Quill, "Sounding Board: Death and Dignity, a Case of Individualized Decision Making," *New England Journal of Medicine* 324: 691–94.

2.	T. E. Quill, B. Lo, and D. W. Brock, "Palliative Options of Last Re-sort: A Comparison of Voluntarily Stopping Eating and Drinking, Terminal Sedation, Physician-Assisted Suicide, and Voluntary Active Euthanasia," *Journal of the American Medical Association* 278 (1997): 2099–104. See also: C. H. Baron, C. Bergstresser, D. W. Brock, et al., "A Model State Act to Authorize and Regulate Physician-Assisted Suicide," *Harvard Journal on Legislation* 33 (1996): 1–34.

3.	Charles Baron, Daniel Brock, Nancy Dorfman, Ed Lowenstein, and Sidney Wanzer constituted a group that met several times in 2005 in an attempt to answer questions about maintaining control of dying in patients who are demented.

4.	I am indebted to Daniel Brock for ideas about this concept. He partic-ipated in the dementia discussion group cited here.

5.	R. Steinbrook, "Physician-Assisted Suicide in Oregon: An Uncertain Future," *New England Journal of Medicine* 346 (2002): 460–64.

CHAPTER 8   WHAT OPTIONS HAVE BEEN USED IN THE PAST TO HASTEN DEATH?

1.	Charles Baron, LLB, PhD (professor of law, Boston College, Boston, MA), in a personal communication with the author, 2003.

2.	Professor Baron stated further, in a personal communication with the author in May 2006: "As regards my position, . . . I think it is danger-ous and counterproductive as well as farcical to play this double effect game. If we leave the matter of whether we are dealing with inten-tional homicide, on the one hand, or just good pain relief, on the other . . . we can neither do an adequate job of protecting against the former or providing room for the latter."

3.	Garrick F. Cole, attorney, Smith & Duggan, Boston, MA, in a per-sonal communication with the author, 2003.

4.	R. McStay, "Terminal Sedation: Palliative Care for Intractable Pain, Post *Glucksberg* and *Quill*," *American Journal of Law and Medicine* 29 (2003): 45–76.

5.	T. Quill, *A Midwife Through the Dying Process: Stories of Healing and Hard Choices at the End of Life* (Baltimore: The Johns Hopkins Uni-versity Press, 1966), 146.

6.	Ann Alpers, "Criminal Act or Palliative Care? Prosecutions Involv-ing the Care of the Dying," *Journal of Law, Medicine & Ethics* 26, 4 (Winter 1998): 308.

7. *State v. Naramore*, 25 Kan. App. 2d 302, 965 P. 2d 211 (1998). The Court of Appeals of Kansas in 1998 heard the case of an osteopathic physician who had been convicted in a lower district court of attempted murder of a terminally ill patient and of intentional and malicious second-degree murder of another terminally ill patient. This conviction was reversed. The physician had used medications for the purpose of treating the patients' symptoms, but he had been charged and convicted in the lower court of motivation to kill the patients.

The court of appeals cited the "physician's impressive array of medical experts that his actions were not homicidal and were medically appropriate" and pointed out that the "burden of proof to establish criminal guilt of a physician for acts arising out of providing medical treatment" is that the criminal guilt must be proved beyond a reasonable doubt, which is the highest standard of proof. The court stated that "we find that no rational jury could find criminal intent and guilt beyond a reasonable doubt based on the record here." There was "strong evidence supporting a reasonable, noncriminal explanation for the doctor's actions. . . . "

The court stated further: "The court has carefully reviewed all the briefs and has done substantial research itself. We can find no criminal conviction of a physician for the attempted murder or murder of a patient which has ever been sustained on appeal based on evidence of the kind presented here."

The court noted the Kansas Medical Society's amicus brief, which discussed the double effect issue: "Palliative care refers to medical intervention in which the primary purpose is to alleviate pain and suffering. It is sometimes referred to as having a 'double effect,' however, because in addition to relieving pain and suffering, the level of pain medication necessary to relieve pain may have the consequence of shortening life. Thus, the health care provider's role as healer conflicts with his or her role as reliever of suffering when increasing amounts of pain medication are required to provide comfort care, but these increasing doses may have the effect of slowing respirations and thereby hastening death. Numerous authorities recognize that cancer patients frequently receive inadequate pain relief."

The same Kansas Medical Society brief also referred to the American Medical Association's Council on Ethical and Judicial Affairs' finding in 1988 that "the administration of a drug necessary to ease the pain of a patient who is terminally ill and suffering excruciating pain may be appropriate treatment even though the effect of the drug may shorten life."

The Kansas Association of Osteopathic Medicine's brief alluded to the problem of physicians' undertreating of pain and summed up: "The modern consensus in medical thinking . . . is a patient's pain *must* be controlled in her terminal illness, even if hastening death is a possible outcome."

The court also made reference to S. H. Wanzer, et al., "The Physician's Responsibility Toward Hopelessly Ill Patients," *New England Journal of Medicine* (1989): 844–47, which stated: "In the patient whose dying process is irreversible, the balance between minimizing pain and suffering and potentially hastening death should be struck clearly in favor of pain relief. Narcotics or other pain medications should be given in whatever dose and by whatever route is necessary for relief."

8. C. F. McKhann, *A Time To Die: The Place for Physician Assistance* (New Haven, CT: Yale University Press, 1998), chapter 5.

9. D. McAulay, "Dehydration in the Terminally Ill Patient," *Nursing Standard* 4 (2001): 33–37.

10. J. Sutcliffe and S. Holmes, "Dehydration: Burden or Benefit to the Dying Patient?" *Journal of Advanced Nursing* 19 (1994): 71–76.

11. R. D. Truog, C. B. Berde, et al., "Barbiturates in the Care of the Terminally Ill," *New England Journal of Medicine* 327 (1992): 1678–82. See also: W. R. Greene and W. H. Davis, "Titrated Intravenous Barbiturates in the Control of Symptoms in Patients with Terminal Cancer," *Southern Medical Journal* 84 (1991): 332–37. See also: N. I. Cherny and R. K. Portenoy, "Sedation in the Management of Refractory Symptoms: Guidelines for Evaluation and Treatment," *Journal of Palliative Care* 10 (1994): 31–38.

12. Details of the pharmacology and preparation of these medications can be obtained in:

    A. *Facts and Comparisons* (St. Louis: Wolters Kluwer Company, 1998),

    B. *American Hospital Formulary Service* (Bethesda: American Society of Health-System Pharmacists, 1998), or

    C. *Handbook on Injectable Drugs*, 8th ed. (Trissel, LA: American Society of Hospital Pharmacists, 1994), 843–49 and 993–98.

The doses suggested in these texts will not be for producing ongoing sedation, but rather for acute use in anesthesia. However, a loading dose short of general anesthesia has been used by physicians to induce unawareness of symptoms, followed by subsequent doses titrated to a level sufficient for ongoing relief of symptoms, usually resulting in a state of somnolence.

13. Personal communication, November 2006, Edward Lowenstein, MD. See also: Medline Plus, U.S. National Library of Medicine, Drugs and Supplements, December 2006, http://www.nlm.nih.gov/medlineplus/druginfo/uspdi/203043.html.

14. R. McStay, "Terminal Sedation: Palliative Care for Intractable Pain, Post *Glucksberg* and *Quill*," *American Journal of Law and Medicine* 29 (2003): 45–76.

15. See, for example, *Brophy v. New England Sinai Hospital*, 398 Mass. 417, 497 N.E.2d 626 (1986), where the Supreme Judicial Court of Massachusetts found a right to refuse artificial nutrition and hydration despite arguments from three dissenting justices that the court had thereby established a right to suicide. Also, even in the context of preservation of prison discipline, such authorizations are no longer the unexceptionable rule. Compare *Singletary v. Costello*, 665 So.2d 1099 (Fla. 1996) and *Thor v. Superior Court*, 855 P.2d 375 (Cal. 1993) with *Laurie v. Senecal*, 666 A.2d 806 (RI 1995).

16. R. A. Burt, "Sounding Board: The Supreme Court Speaks—Not Assisted Suicide but a Constitutional Right to Palliative Care," *New England Journal of Medicine* 337 (1997): 1234. Also, note that in 1997 the U.S. Supreme Court ruled unanimously in the cases of *Washington v. Glucksberg* and *Vacco v. Quill* that there was not a constitutional right to assisted suicide, and the court as a whole did not directly consider voluntary refusal of hydration. However, individual justices acknowledged considerations that may fairly be seen as supportive of the procedure. Specifically, the chief justice, writing for the court as a whole, acknowledged in *Glucksberg* that a state may not force medical care upon a dying patient for the purpose of keeping the patient alive: "A person has a constitutionally protected liberty interest in refusing unwanted medical treatment. . . . The U.S. Constitution would grant a competent person a constitutionally protected right to refuse lifesaving hydration and nutrition." In addition, the opinions of Justices

O'Connor, Breyer, Ginsburg, and Stevens in *Glucksberg* and in *Quill* support the right of the patient to have his or her symptoms relieved by effective medication. See, for example, Cal. Bus. & Prof. Code §2241.5 (West 1994); Fla. Stat. Ann. §458.326 (West 1995); Mo. Ann. Stat. §§334.105 et seq. (Vernon 1995); Nev. Rev. Stat. §630.3066 (1995); N.D. Cent. Code (West 1996); and Va. Code Ann. §54.1–3408.1 (Michie 1995).

17. See, for example, Cal. Bus. & Prof. Code §2241.5 (West 1994); Fla. Stat. Ann. §458.326 (West 1995); Mo. Ann. Stat. §§334.105 et seq. (Vernon 1995); Nev. Rev. Stat. §630.3066 (1995); N.D. Cent. Code (West 1996); and Va. Code Ann. §54.1–3408.1 (Michie 1995).

18. D. Humphry, *Final Exit*, 1991, New York: Dell Publishing.

19. D. Humphry, *Final Exit: The Practicalities of Self-Deliverance and Assisted Suicide for the Dying*, 3rd ed. (New York: Dell Trade Paperback, 2002) ISBN 0385 336 535. Can be ordered from ERGO! 24829 Norris Lane, Junction City, OR 97448-9559.

20. Oregon Department of Human Services, 800 NE Oregon St., Portland, OR 97232. Web site http://www.dhs.state.or.us/publichealth /chs/pas/ar-index.cfm. See appendix for *Fifth Annual Report on Oregon's Death with Dignity Act*.

21. Derek Humphry recommends in his book that one may use a plastic bag over the head in addition to the drugs—to induce a lack of oxygen and thereby be certain that the death from the barbiturates occurs relatively speedily. Many persons are put off by the idea of the bag. If the dose of the barbiturate is nine grams and if it is taken quickly so the whole dose is ingested before sleep supervenes, the use of the bag has seemed to most physicians to be unnecessary. If a patient takes longer than the average to die, it is still not a prolonged event, and the patient (completely asleep) is unaware of anything after the first few minutes. Observers have noted that end-of-life events in which helium is utilized in a bag-like hood for the purpose of delivering the helium are another matter. The hood is necessary to deliver the helium to the patient, but it is tent-like and not constricting around the face.

22. As is commonly known by doctors in Oregon and in many countries, one hour before the barbiturate is ingested, the beta-blocker propranolol has been taken orally, producing an anti-adrenaline effect that slows the heartrate and lowers the blood pressure. It's helpfulness is

questionable. At the same time, medication has been taken orally to promote rapid emptying of the stomach (so the barbiturate can be more quickly absorbed into the bloodstream), and anti-nausea medication has been used to reduce the likelihood of vomiting.

23. The following are examples of several states in which the prohibition is particularly daunting.

- Montana code annotated, title 45, Crimes; Chapter 5, offenses against the person; Part 1, homicide; 45-5-105, aiding or soliciting suicide: "A person who purposely aids or solicits another to commit suicide, but such suicide does not occur, commits the offense of aiding or soliciting suicide. A person convicted of the offense of aiding or soliciting a suicide shall be imprisoned in the state prison for any term not to exceed 10 years or be fined an amount not to exceed $50,000, or both. . . . If the conduct of the offender made him the agent of the death, the offense is criminal homicide, notwithstanding the consent or even the solicitations of the victim. . . . The rationale behind the felony sentence for the substantive offense of aiding or soliciting suicide is that the act typifies a very low regard for human life."

- Michigan compiled laws annotated; chapter XLV, homicide; 750.329a: "A person who knows that an individual intends to kill himself or herself and does any of the following with the intent to assist the individual in killing himself or herself is guilty of criminal assistance to the killing of an individual, a felony punishable by imprisonment for not more than 5 years or a fine of not more than $10,000, or both:

A. provides the means by which the individual attempts to kill himself or herself or kills himself or herself,

B. participates in an act by which the individual attempts to kill himself or herself or kills himself or herself,

C. helps the individual plan to attempt to kill himself or herself or to kill himself or herself.

    This section does not apply to withholding or withdrawing medical treatment."

- Louisiana revised statutes, Title 14, criminal law; chapter 1, criminal code; Part II, offenses against the person; Subpart A-2, suicide: "Criminal assistance to suicide is:
    1. The intentional advising or encouraging of another person to commit suicide or the providing of the physical means or *the knowledge of such means* [author's emphasis] to another person for the purpose of enabling the other person to commit or attempt to commit suicide.
    2. The intentional advising, encouraging, or assisting of another person to commit suicide, or the participation in any physical act which causes, aids, abets, or assists another person in committing or attempting to commit suicide."

24. L. Schafer, "The Dearth of Choices," *EOL Choices* 1 (2002): 15.

CHAPTER 9 HELIUM: NEWLY USED METHOD TO END SUFFERING

1. The great majority of topics addressed in this book I know of from personal experience—simply living through the era of vast changes in end-of-life management. The recent use of helium to hasten death is an exception, because this came about after I ceased my medical practice. Information in this chapter on this subject comes from conversations with colleagues who are personally knowledgeable about the subject and whose judgment and accuracy I trust.

2. R. Ogden and R. Wooten, "Asphyxial Suicide with Helium and a Plastic Bag," *American Journal of Forensic Medicine and Pathology* 23 (2002): 234–37.

3. The use of helium to end life has been described in detail in Derek Humphry's *Final Exit: The Practicalities of Self-Deliverance and Assisted Suicide for the Dying*, 3rd ed. (New York: Dell Trade, 2002–03), obtainable at Euthanasia Research & Guidance Organization (ERGO), 24829 Norris Lane, Junction City, OR 97448. This forty-six-minute DVD of *Final Exit* is available from www.finalexit.org/ergo-store. These sources describe what some people have done in the last few years to end suffering.

4. Faye Girsh, EdD, *World Right-To-Die Newsletter, News and Archives, World News and Research Updates*, April 22, 2004, reported on the use of helium in a summary, "The Many Ways to Hasten Death." She de-

scribed the efforts being taken on the world scene to find the ideal way of ending suffering, www.worldrtd.net/news/world/?id=665.

5. Much of the information in this section comes from Derek Humphry's writings and videos. See note 3 in this chapter. He has kindly given me permission to use this information in this section.

CHAPTER 10   DIFFERENTIATING SADNESS AT THE END OF LIFE FROM CLINICAL DEPRESSION

1. American Psychiatric Association, *Diagnostic and Statistical Manual of Mental Disorders*, 4th ed., Text Revision (Washington, DC: American Psychiatric Press, 2000), 349–56.
2. Ibid.

CHAPTER 11   THE SPECIAL CASE OF IRREVERSIBLE DEMENTIA AND END-OF-LIFE MANAGEMENT

1. This discussion group consisted of Charles Baron, professor of law at Boston College; Dan Brock, PhD, professor of medical ethics in the department of social medicine, director of the division of medical ethics at Harvard Medical School, and director of the Harvard University Program in Ethics and Health; Nancy Dorfman, PhD, recent president of Compassion and Choices of Greater Boston; Edward Lowenstein, MD, professor of medical ethics, Harvard Medical School; and the author.
2. The idea of the present self precommitting the future self first came to my attention through personal communication with Daniel Brock in 2005. His ideas have been published: D. Brock "Precommitment in Bioethics: Some Theoretical Issues," *Texas Law Review*, June 2003; Symposium: Precommitment Theory in Bioethics and Constitutional Law Bioethics.
3. M. F. Mendez and J. L. Cummings, *Dementia, A Clinical Approach*, 3rd ed. (New York: Butterworth-Heinemann, 2003).
4. Alzheimer's Association, 225 N. Michigan Ave., Fl. 17, Chicago, IL 60601-7633, 800-272-3900, www.alz.org.
5. M. F. Mendez and J. L. Cummings. *Dementia, A Clinical Approach*, 3rd ed. (New York: Butterworth-Heinemann, 2003), 3–4.
6. Lowenstein, Edward, MD, in a private communication with the author, May 2005.

CHAPTER 13 ALLOWING A MERCIFUL DEATH

1. J. Fensterman, "I See Why Others Choose to Die," *Boston Globe*, Op-ed page, January 31, 2006.
2. PRNewswire, Rochester, NY, April 27, 2005, cited by ERGO, righttodie2@mailman.efn.org.
3. D. E. Lee, "Physician-Assisted Suicide: A Conservative Critique of Intervention," *Hastings Center Report* 33 (2003): 17–19.
4. J. Feinberg, *Social Philosophy* (Englewood Cliffs, NJ: Prentice-Hall, 1973), 49–51.
5. There have been efforts in recent years to pass Oregon-like laws in other states. California, Hawaii, Maine, and Vermont have all put on strong campaigns for such a law, but none as yet has succeeded. Vermont advocates are cautiously optimistic for 2007, and favorable action in California is very possible. Once one more state passes a law of this sort, more states will probably follow.

APPENDIX A HISTORICAL BACKGROUND OF THE END-OF-LIFE MOVEMENT AND CURRENT NATIONAL ORGANIZATIONS

1. Sidney Rosoff, in a personal communication with the author, November 4, 2002.
2. D. Humphry, *Final Exit: The Practicalities of Self-Deliverance and Assisted Suicide for the Dying* 3rd ed., 2004, with 2005 addendum. Available at http://ergo-store.finalexit.org.
3. *Frequently Asked Questions About Hemlock Society USA*, leaflet, 2003. The Hemlock Society USA, P.O. Box 101810, Denver, CO 80250-1810.
4. Compassion in Dying Web site, 2002, www.CompassioninDying.org.
5. *Using the Oregon Death with Dignity Act: A Guide for Physicians* (Portland: Compassion in Dying of Oregon, 2000).
6. ERGO Newsletter, January 31, 2005.
7. Barbara Coombs Lee, president and CEO of Compassion in Dying), in a personal communication with the author, December 9, 2002.
8. Compassion and Choices newsletter, March 2005.
9. Final Exit Network, 2005 mailing to members.
10. T. Goodwin, president of the Final Exit Network, e-mail, January 21, 2006, info@finalexitnetwork.org.

11. Death with Dignity National Center Web site, www.deathwithdignity.org, accessed April 27, 2005.
12. Derek Humphry, in a personal communication with the author, 2005.

Appendix C   The International Scene

1. C. Nickerson, "Suicide groups make Switzerland a final destination," *Boston Globe*, February 27, 2006.
2. ERGO Newsletter, April 22, 2005.
3. Nickerson, "Suicide groups make Switzerland a final destination."
4. The World Federation of Right to Die Societies, www.worldrtd.net/news/world/?id=603, October 1, 2003.
5. Georg Bosshad, Esther Ulrich, and Walter Bär, of the University of Zurich's Institute of Legal Medicine, published in the *Swiss Medical Weekly* 133 (2003): 310–17.
6. ERGO Newsletter, December 17, 2004.
7. Dying with Dignity pamphlet, 2006. Dying with Dignity, 55 Eglinton Avenue East, Suite 802, Toronto, Ontario M4P 1G8.
8. Richard MacDonald, MD, former president of the World Federation of Right to Die Societies, personal communication.

Appendix G   Proposed Authorization for Ending Life in Situations of Irreversible and Progressive Cognitive Decline

1. Many of the points in this special advance directive for Alzheimer patients are based on an Alzheimer living will originally created by End of Life Choices Arizona in 2004 and subsequently modified by Faye Girsh.

INDEX

Addictions. *See under* Medications
Advance directives, 5, 83, 86, 96,
    137, 141–148
  absence of, 147
  See also Living wills; Medical
    proxies
Alpers, Ann, 95–96
Alzheimer Association, 133
Alzheimer's disease, 1, 3, 10, 11,
    82–83, 131, 133–134, 146.
    See also Dementia
*American Journal of Law and
    Medicine*, 101
American Medical Association
    Code of Medical Ethics, 46
American Psychiatric Association,
    128
Angell, Marcia, 151
Antibiotics, 10, 21, 30, 137
Anxiety, 28, 44, 52, 76, 112, 126
Ashcroft, John, 110
Autonomy, 7, 15, 82, 86

Barbiturates, 13, 76–77, 91, 100,
    103–113, 122
  availability of, 110–111
  ingested as a powder, 107
  lethal dose of, 107, 126

secrecy regarding use of,
    111–113
shelf life of, 108
See also Legal issues, legality of
    barbiturate use
Baron, Charles and Irma, 67–69,
    93
Belgium, 152
Breathlessness, 4, 27–28

Canada, 110
Cancer, 7, 23–24, 28, 39, 49, 56,
    58–59, 61, 68, 69, 75, 76,
    103, 104, 125–126, 128
Carbon dioxide, 117, 119
Carbon monoxide, 89–90
Cardiopulmonary resuscitation
    (CPR), 17, 30. *See also* Do-
    not-resuscitate order
Catholic Church, 6
Chemotherapy, 24, 40, 56, 68
Clinical depression, 81–82
  vs. sadness at end of life,
    125–129
  symptoms of, 127–128
Codeine category drugs, 50, 53
Cole, Garrick F., 93
Comfort care. *See* Palliative care

Acknowledgments

I wish to thank the many persons who helped me with this book.

Joseph Glenmullen urged me to undertake the project and then collaborated with me in the preparation, organization, and editing of the book. A former colleague of mine at the Harvard University Health Services during a ten-year period, we practiced together, he in psychiatry and I in internal medicine. His advice and friendship have been invaluable.

The late Florence Clothier Wislocki, MD, initially got me involved in end-of-life issues in the 1960s when we fought together for living-will legislation in Massachusetts. She paved the way for my going on the board of the Society for the Right-to-Die, where my association with the wonderful activists in that group began. Specifically, the late Joseph Fletcher, PhD, author of *Situation Ethics*, was a role model for me in my conversion to espousing physician aid-in-dying and euthanasia. Another in the Society for the Right-to-Die whose influence and friendship remain with me to this day is Sidney Rosoff, president of that organization and later of the Hemlock Society and World Federation of Right to Die Societies. Alice Mehling, dogged executive director of the Right to Die Society gave me important help in the early years, as did board members Ruth Smith and Bry Benjamin.

In more recent years, Derek Humphry was an inspiring leader as the founder of the Hemlock Society and continues to the present to give wise counsel. Faye Girsh gave me her overall encouragement, friendship, and support in end-of-life issues over the past two decades, and she allowed me to use in the book a modified version of her patients' statement of wishes regarding Alzheimer's disease care at the end of life, which, in turn, had been based partially on an

Alzheimer statement prepared by the Arizona chapter of End-of-Life Choices. Richard MacDonald, MD, former medical director at the Hemlock Society and its successor organization, Compassion and Choices, and most recently a senior medical advisor to the Final Exit Network, has been an ever gracious and kind source of answers for my frequent questions, and I admire his courage and dedication in the work he has so generously given this whole movement. Charles Baron, professor of law at Boston College, and Garrick Cole, a Boston attorney—both of whom are clear-thinking experts in the legal intricacies of end-of-life care—were colleagues with me in the development of a model law for physician aid-in-dying, and they have given their time and advice to me through the years. They are good friends. Many of these persons also reviewed sections of the book and made excellent suggestions.

Ruth Porter, valued nurse practitioner colleague of mine in private practice, was a true ally in trying to care properly for dying patients. Russell Butler, MD, a neurologist colleague of mine in Massachusetts, has given important help to the movement through the years. William Comer, pharmacist, has through the years kindly discussed with me various pharmacological questions. I learned much from the late James Vorenburg, professor of law and dean of the Harvard Law School, who collaborated on several end-of-life projects. Harvey Silverglate rendered invaluable advice about legal issues. Nancy Dorfman, president of the Boston right-to-die group, has been a steadfast friend and colleague in this field for many years, and she reviewed the statement of wishes pertaining to the possibility of cognitive decline. Barbara Coombs Lee, president and co-CEO of Compassion and Dying, has given freely of her support and advice, and Lois Schafer at the Compassion and Dying headquarters in Denver gave me assistance in thinking about living wills. N. Cody Webb, MD, has been a friend in the movement through many years and a never-failing source of information. S. James Adelstein, MD, collaborated in the 1980s with me in the creation of two articles about the physician's responsibility toward hopelessly ill patients, and has been a close friend and wise counsel for over fifty years. Daniel Federman, MD, at Harvard Medical School, was critical to the success of the same project regarding hopelessly ill patients. Edwin Cassem, MD, also was an important contributor to that project. Eli Stutsman kindly reviewed material for me and made suggestions. Alan Meisel, JD, University of Pittsburgh, gave helpful advice regarding physician risks in certain circumstances. Daniel Brock, PhD, medical ethicist, has helped me a number of times in my thinking on end-of-life problems. Larry Egbert, MD, provided important support in this project on several occasions. Edward Lowenstein, MD, the Reverend Ralph Mero, and Richard Walters all gave me good assistance for which I am grateful.

There are many other unnamed medical colleagues of mine who have been leaders and allies in the evolution of the death-with-dignity movement.

Merloyd Lawrence has been the Perseus/Da Capo editor for the book. In a word, she has been wonderful in every way. There was hardly ever a suggestion with which I did not agree. Robert Lescher, our literary agent, was of invaluable help in guiding us to Merloyd.

Anne, my dear wife and principal sounding board, helped me with her ideas through many drafts and was my common-sense anchor for the book.

Lastly, and importantly, I thank those patients of mine and their families who allowed me to use their stories in this book.

Sidney H. Wanzer, MD
January 2007

About the Authors

SIDNEY WANZER, MD, a nationally recognized authority on issues of death and dying, learned what did and did not work in end-of-life treatment in almost four decades of internal medicine, initially in private practice and later with the Harvard University Health Services. He was the lead author of the groundbreaking article in the *New England Journal of Medicine* which for the first time held that, in certain situations, it could be ethical for a physician to assist in hastening the death of patients suffering intolerably. The current president of the Boston chapter of Compassion and Choices, he lives in Concord, Massachusetts and has three grown children and six grandchildren.

JOSEPH GLENMULLEN, MD, Clinical Instructor in Psychiatry at Harvard Medical School, is on the staff of Harvard University Health Services and in private practice in Cambridge, Massachusetts. His works include the widely praised *Prozac Backlash* and *The Antidepressant Solution*.